CORNELL STUDIES IN ENGLISH
VOLUME XXXV

EDITED BY
LANE COOPER

Plato and Milton

BY IRENE SAMUEL

Plato's thought is built into the ethics of Milton's poems as substantially as some parts of the Bible are built into their plots.

MERRITT Y. HUGHES, *John Milton, 'Paradise Regained,' the Minor Poems, and 'Samson Agonistes,'* p. 411.

How little the commentators of Milton have availed themselves of the writings of Plato, Milton's darling! SAMUEL TAYLOR COLERIDGE, Letter to W. Sotheby, September 10, 1802.

Next to Homer and the inspired Hebrew poets, no author exercised a more powerful influence on the congenial sublimity of Milton's genius than Plato.

BENJAMIN JOWETT, 'The Genius of Plato,' *Edinburgh Review* 87 (1848). 335.

PLATO *and* MILTON

IRENE SAMUEL

Associate Professor of English at Hunter College

CORNELL UNIVERSITY PRESS

ITHACA, NEW YORK

Contents

TO LANE COOPER

Late Professor of the English Language
and Literature in Cornell University

Preface

No one, to my knowledge, has ever doubted that Milton knew the Dialogues and Epistles of Plato—along with very nearly everything else a man of his time might read. Indeed, a list of those who have written, cursorily or at length, of the relation between the two men might be extended far beyond the one appended to this volume. But in spite of the liberal use of Plato in annotated texts of Milton, and even after the work of Dr. Herbert Agar on *Milton and Plato*, the extent to which Milton accepted Platonic teaching has still to be appraised.

My own work began with the study of Plato. Coming to Milton with the Dialogues and Epistles fresh in mind, I could not read *Paradise Lost* and *Paradise Regained* as Puritan poems, nor see Milton as a mere Satanic rebel. Everywhere in his work there were echoes of Plato, many that might have come from intermediate sources, some of them Christian, but many, too, that only a close reading of Plato by Milton himself could produce. Whoever wishes may cull three shoe-boxes of such parallels; I wished to, and did, in my graduate study at Cornell University. For my doctoral dissertation, written under the direction of Professor Lane Cooper, I used only the passages from Milton's poems—one boxful. My notes on the Platonic origins of those passages are available on pages 258-386 of a type-written dissertation entitled *Platonism in the Poetry of John Milton*.

In the present study, the reader has been spared the notes. Early in the collection of them it became clear that the works of Plato had been not merely a source, but a stimulant, to Milton, and had acted as a catalytic agent on the heterogeneous materials of pagan, Biblical, and Christian learning in his mind. Moreover, the Platonic pattern into which these materials were fused seemed to explain some troublesome questions about the poems of Milton. The apparently inconsistent treatment of knowledge in *Areopagitica* and *Paradise Lost,* the paradox of Adam's fall, the discrepant rejection and use of the pagan classics in *Paradise Regained;* these and the like questions resolved themselves when held to the light of Plato's thought.

Lest the pattern here traced seem strained to my reader, I have devoted the first two chapters to a factual account of Milton as a student of Plato and Platonists. Of his unconscious or 'native' Platonism I can pretend to no knowledge. Certainly much of his Platonizing, especially in early works, was derivative, and certainly he did not check every thought that entered his head against the canon of Plato. But his assimilation of Platonic teaching was reasonably conscious.

In the light, then, of Milton's avowed study of Plato I have sought to explain the poetic and ethical theories that underlie *Paradise Lost, Paradise Regained,* and, less ostensibly since it is a less discursive poem, *Samson Agonistes.* I have followed the argument where it led, and, I trust, duly acknowledged the fact when it led beyond Plato. Although no appraisal of Milton's Christian doctrine is attempted, the reader will see that Milton takes his place, along with Augustine and Dean Inge, among Christian Platonists. He is also, like Spenser and Shelley, a Platonic poet; and it is thus that he here concerns us. Plato did not affect Milton precisely as he affected Shelley or Spenser; for the effect of any writer varies with the reader. But the use Milton made of Plato can tell us much about the relation between a philosopher and a poet, and perhaps even about that between a poet's philosophy and his poetry.

It is, at any rate, in that hope that I offer the following pages. For the sake of readability I have reduced the footnotes to a minimum; used translations for most passages in Greek, Latin, and Italian; in the main normalized the spelling and punctuation of Milton's prose; and in general tried to give the results and conceal the process of research. The editions and translations employed in the text are given in the List of References to Publications on pp. 173-175. I wish here to acknowledge my indebtedness to the following publishers and persons for permission to quote from works in their copyright: the Macmillan Company for Milton's *Private Correspondence and Academic Exercises* translated by Phyllis B. Tillyard, Augustine's *De Civitate Dei* edited by J. E. C. Welldon, *The English Grammar Schools to 1660* by Foster Watson; the Oxford University Press and the Clarendon Press for the edition and translation of the *Hermetica* by Walter Scott, the translations by Lane Cooper of Plato's dialogues on art, by Benjamin Jowett of *The Dialogues of Plato,* and by W. W. Jackson of Dante's *Convivio;* E. P. Dutton and Company for *The Republic of Plato* translated by A. D. Lindsay; Jackson, Son and Company for *The Sonnets of Milton* edited and translated by John S. Smart; the Odyssey Press for the Preface to an edition of Milton's poems by Merritt Y. Hughes; the Princeton University Press for *Milton and Plato* by Herbert Agar; the University of Michigan Press and Professor James Holly Hanford for his essay on 'The Youth of Milton' in *Studies in Shakespeare, Milton, and Donne;* and the Columbia University Press for *The Works of John Milton,* from which most of my quotations from Milton's prose works are taken. I have also to thank the editors of *Studies in Philology* for permission to use in modified form as the first chapter of this book my article on 'Milton's References to Plato and Socrates,' which appeared in that periodical. Mr. Herbert Agar gave me permission in 1939 to use his *Milton and Plato* as the starting point of my work.

Most of this study had been written before I read C. S. Lewis's *Preface to Paradise Lost,* and all of it before the work of Douglas Bush, *'Paradise Lost' in Our Time,* appeared. But I am indebted to both volumes for confirming me in views independently arrived at. My work owes much to the encouragement and advice of my teachers, Professor Lane Cooper and Professor Charles W. Jones of Cornell University, and of Professor John S. Diekhoff, formerly my colleague at Queens College. Among other friends who have helped me in ways too numerous to list, I wish especially to thank Dr. Mary Campbell Brill for her careful and generous assistance in proof-reading and compiling the Index.

IRENE SAMUEL

Hunter College
1946

Plato and Milton

CHAPTER I

Milton as a Student of Plato

THE DOCTRINE which we find in the writings of John Milton shows an unusual degree of consistency; and while in a mind as complex as his, consistency is not sameness, we may draw from his work the principles that generally guided his thought. They do not belong to any one philosophical system. Indeed, a man of his endowment and learning necessarily agrees with some part of most systems; the better part, we may suppose. But the correspondence between his doctrine and that of Plato is remarkably close; moreover, as we shall see, we have Milton's own warrant for thinking the correspondence important.

In order to appraise the influence of one writer on another, we must start, of course, from explicit references. But we need not take a narrow view of the transmission of thought from mind to mind. Only a pedant would lift word after word from another's page, or retain in separate compartments of his mind what he has learned from this source and what from that. A thought once assimilated will readily flow into channels far from its original source. Thus, if Milton truly accepts some definite view from Plato, he is not likely to tag it at every use, much less to name the dialogue or epistle in which he found it. In large part the effect of a writer upon any reader cannot be traced back to isolated passages; the spirit of the whole is more likely to remain with him than a series of excerpts.

Both sympathy and caution must, therefore, guide the interpreter. To the commentators who name the Cabala as a primary source of Milton's thought, we may fairly object that they show little caution, since his one reference to this 'source' is a disparaging use of the term 'Cabalists' in *Eikonoclastes* (5.252). Conversely, Dr. Herbert Agar shows too much caution, and too little sympathy, when, after finding the Platonic origin of many passages in the works of Milton, he hesitates to assert that 'Plato's effect upon Milton's thought, or upon his spiritual development, was of major importance.' Milton did assert it.

In the year 1642, looking back over his past in order to answer a libelous attack on his conduct, he reviewed the course of his reading. He said in effect: This is what my mind fed on, and feeding on this, it reached these decisions; how could I then have acted as my accuser says? Apparently he believed that knowledge determines choice, and therefore offered his doctrine as a proof of his character, and his literary preferences as a proof of his doctrine. Whether or not the argument was of a kind to convince opponents, it provides a key to the mind of the man who used it. And Plato is a part of that key; here Milton spoke unmistakably:

Thus, from the laureate fraternity of poets, riper years and the ceaseless round of study and reading led me to the shady spaces of philosophy, but chiefly to the divine volumes of Plato and his equal Xenophon: where, if I should tell ye what I learned of chastity and love, I mean that which is truly so, whose charming cup is only virtue, which she bears in her hand to those who are worthy (the rest are cheated with a thick intoxicating potion, which a certain sorceress, the abuser of love's name, carries about), and how the first and chiefest office of love begins and ends in the soul, producing those happy twins of her divine generation, knowledge and virtue, with such abstracted sublimities as these, it might be worth your listening, readers,

4

as I may one day hope to have ye in a still time, when there shall be no chiding. (3. 305.)[1]

To be sure, this passage in the *Apology for Smectymnuus* looks backward, and is concerned with a doctrine of love. How much more of its author does it reveal, and for how long a period? How much of the thought of Plato, moreover, do the words allude to? The references Milton made to Plato and Socrates answer these questions.

Now such references are, of course, hardly a matter for surprise. An Englishman of the seventeenth century, trained at St. Paul's and Cambridge, at home in the academies of Italy, and in correspondence with the learned men of his time, who had *not* found occasion to mention Plato and Socrates would astonish us. And Milton, before he entered school at the age of twelve, had already studied languages with Thomas Young. The curriculum at St. Paul's, from what we know of its founders and its headmaster in Milton's time, Alexander Gill, doubtless included selections from Plato.[2] We may surmise from the popular handbook of Erasmus, *De Duplici Copia rerum ac verborum Commentarii duo,* that schoolboys of the Renaissance knew parts, at least, of Plato's *Symposium, Apology, Crito, Phaedo,* and *Republic,* as well as the Socratic writings of Xenophon, Cebes' *Picture of Human Life,* and the fragment of Aeschines—all perhaps in translation. Milton, we know, thought reading like this suited to young students; he must have had in mind when he wrote *Of Education* his own happy years at St. Paul's. He may even have read in the headmaster's *Logonomia Anglica* (p. 83) this English and Latin illustration of the superlative de-

---

[1] The numbers in parenthesis, when no other source is indicated, refer to the Columbia edition of *The Works of John Milton.*

[2] See J. H. Lupton, *Life of Dean Colet,* pp. 168-9, 171; Foster Watson, *The English Grammar Schools to 1660;* and Arthur Barker, 'Milton's Schoolmasters,' *MLR.* 32 (1937). 517-36.

5

gree: 'Among ðe Filosoferz, Plato was ðe most lerned; *inter Philosophos Plato doctissimus fuit.*' And he may have had to debate a question like that which John Clarke recorded among *Quaestiones aliquot declamatoriae* at the Lincoln Grammar-School: '*Utrum utilius sit Socratem de moribus quam Hippocratem de humoribus disputantem audire.*'[3]

In any case, Milton had learned something of Plato and his master at St. Paul's, had heard them praised, and probably used only a commonplace of the schools when he addressed Thomas Young in his Fourth *Elegy:*

> Carior ille mihi quam tu, doctissime Graium,
> Cliniadi, pronepos qui Telamonis erat;
> Quamque Stagirites generoso magnus alumno,
> Quem peperit Libyco Chaonis alma Iovi.

Clearly, he had not yet studied Plato intensively.

Did he reach 'the shady spaces of philosophy' at Christ's College? His undergraduate writings contain several allusions to Socrates and Plato. In his Second *Prolusion* (12. 150), Plato is '*ille Naturae Matris optimus interpres*' for describing the Sirens on the edge of each sphere, and Aristotle is '*Pythagorae et Platonis aemulus et perpetuus Calumniator.*' We read in the Sixth *Prolusion:*

> Moreover Socrates, according to the Pythian Apollo the wisest of men, is said often to have bridled his wife's shrewish tongue with a jesting word. Besides, we read that the conversation of the ancient philosophers was always sprinkled with witty sayings and enlivened by a pleasant sparkle. (Tillyard, pp. 90-1.)[4]

And again:

> We too keep the custom of amusing ourselves as Socrates advised. (*Ibid.*, p. 98.)

---

[3] See Watson, *op. cit.*, pp. 454, 466.

[4] The translations of Milton's letters and prolusions are taken from Phyllis B. Tillyard, *Milton, Private Correspondence and Academic Exercises.*

In the Seventh *Proclusion,* Milton derides *'illud nescire Socraticum,'* but speaks with delight of conferences

such as those which the divine Plato is said often to have held in the shade of that famous plane-tree, conversations which all mankind might well have flocked to hear in spell-bound silence. (*Ibid.,* p. 111.)

But these remarks may all be as conventional as that in the Fourth *Elegy.* In Milton's age, as in ours, a good many persons doubtless referred to Plato and Socrates even among those who knew little more of the one than that he might be called divine and of the other that he was called the wisest of men. The references to Plato and Socrates in Milton's Academic Exercises and Elegies might have come from any one of similar training. They are vague, reveal no special insight into the teaching of Plato, and have no close tie to their writer's own belief. The like may be said of the verses *De Idea Platonica,* whenever they were composed. The lines show some knowledge and some affection, but even their 'sportive' tone and the precedent of Renaissance Platonism hardly excuse Milton for accepting Hermes Trismegistus as a valid interpreter of Platonic thought.[5] So too with *Il Penseroso,* where Plato is to be unsphered for such work as had better been left to 'thrice-great Hermes':

> Or let my Lamp at midnight hour,
> Be seen in some high lonely Tow'r,
> Where I may oft out-watch the Bear,
> With thrice-great Hermes, or unsphere
> The spirit of Plato to unfold
> What Worlds, or what vast Regions hold
> The immortal mind that hath forsook
> Her mansion in this fleshly nook:

---

[5] Cf. W. Skeat and E. H. Visiak, *Milton's Lament for Damon and His Other Latin Poems,* p. 66; and Walter Mac Kellar, *The Latin Poems of John Milton,* pp. 17, 51-3.

And of those Daemons that are found
In fire, air, flood, or under ground,
Whose power hath a true consent
With Planet, or with Element. (85-96.)[6]

Such words reflect a contemporary enthusiasm, but reveal little independent study. Evidently the name of Plato had long been impressed upon Milton as that of an eminent, perhaps the most eminent, philosopher; and though Milton was seldom content to take impressions at second hand, Plato had not yet begun to exercise a determinant influence upon him.

The verses added by Milton to the Seventh *Elegy* when he published his Latin poems in 1645 confirm the conventionality of his earlier Platonism:

These vain trophies of my idleness I once set up in foolish mood and with supine endeavor. Injurious error, forsooth, led me astray, and untutored youth was a bad teacher; until the shady Academy offered its Socratic streams, and freed me from the yoke to which I had submitted. At once these flames were extinguished, and thenceforth my breast has been stiff with encircling ice, whence Cupid has feared a frost for his arrows, and Venus fears my Diomedean strength! (Mac Kellar, p. 107.)[7]

This recantation has an evident purpose. At a definite time in Milton's life, we are to understand, Plato with his Socratic teaching profoundly altered the poet's habit of thought. And this difference in emphasis is what chiefly distinguishes the Platonizing of the early works from that zest for Plato which began at some definite period in Milton's 'riper years'; the account of his education in the

---

[6] Cf. E. C. Baldwin, 'A Note on *Il Penseroso,' MLN.* 33 (1918). 184-5. Quotations from Milton's English poems are taken from the text of H. J. C. Grierson, *The Poems of John Milton,* except where another source is indicated.

[7] The translations of Milton's Latin poems are taken from Walter Mac Kellar, *The Latin Poems of John Milton.*

Apology, and the late postscript to the Seventh *Elegy,* assert the influence of Plato on Milton's *ethical* theory, and particularly on his theory of love. The Platonic citations and allusions in the Academic Exercises, the Latin poems, and *Il Penseroso,* while in all probability drawn from the Dialogues, nowhere indicate that those Dialogues have a central and unifying doctrine. The music of the spheres, the conference under the plane-tree, the Socratic sportiveness and pretended ignorance, the idea distinct from phenomena, the immortal mind freed of its 'fleshly nook,' all these are related to a view of human life with which Milton's early writings were scarcely concerned.

No such doubt can touch his letter to Charles Diodati, dated from London, September 23, 1637:

> Though I know not God's intent toward me in other respects, yet of this I am sure, that he has imbued me especially with a mighty passion for Beauty. Ceres never sought her daughter Proserpine (as the legend tells) with greater ardor than I do this Idea of Beauty, like some image of loveliness; ever pursuing it, by day and by night, in every shape and form ('for many forms there are of things divine') and following close in its footprints as it leads. And so, whensover I find one who spurns the base opinions of common men, and dares to be, in thought and word and deed, that which the wisest minds throughout the ages have approved; whensoever, I say, I find such a man, to him I find myself impelled forthwith to cleave. And if I am fated, either by nature or destiny, never to attain this high honor and glory in my own proper person, for all my toil and striving, yet sure I am that neither god nor man shall forbid me to honor and revere all my days those who have won such glory as this, or are happily striving toward it.
>
> To change the subject, I know it is time to satisfy your curiosity. You make many eager enquiries, even asking about my thoughts. I will tell you, Diodati, but let me whisper it in your ear, to spare my blushes, and allow me for a moment to speak to you in a boastful strain. What am I thinking about? you ask. So help me God, of immortality. What am I doing? Growing

wings and learning to fly; but my Pegasus can only rise on tender pinions as yet, so let my new wisdom be humble. (Tillyard, p. 14.)

This is Milton's first intimate use of Plato. Though *Phaedrus* is not named, Diodati is expected to place the allusion and understand the Platonic language. Evidently Milton had known an Italian Platonist before ever he entered an *accademia*. And the whole passage differs from the commonplaces of school and society on the Idea of the Beautiful. Here is no mistress praised as the very incarnation of that glorious idea, but a friend is told that he, but not he alone, is loved because this Idea of Beauty leaves its print on many shapes and forms, and especially on the spirit of an uncommonly good man. The friend is even told his use; by his aid the soul grows its wings to its own end, immortality, that it may have vision of the very 'image of loveliness,' and fly its Pegasus, if it be the soul of a poet, to the rim of heaven itself. Here is that love 'which is truly so,' the doctrine that Milton thought among the most important sources of his essential education. Here is the authentic note of ardent Platonism.

But was it the first time Milton sounded that note? *Comus,* written three years earlier, contains a similar paraphrase, from *Phaedo* 81. And surely much in *Comus* comes from the Dialogues, and much is ardent. Still, is its Platonizing exactly Platonic? Coleridge thought so, and most commentators since have found the Mask the most Platonic of Milton's works. Hanford suggests a more likely explanation: 'That a poet should be a poet's guide to emotional Platonism is very natural. That Spenser should have been the guide of Milton is particularly so.'[8] Put the question thus: Is the conversation of the Mask such a dialogue as Plato might have written on the subject, or

---

[8] James Holly Hanford, 'The Youth of Milton,' in *Studies in Shakespeare, Milton, and Donne*, p. 139.

the saintly Lady a second Diotima versed in the deep mysteries of Love? Surely no more than Comus with his bestiality resembles the Aristophanes created by Plato. The theories of the Mask, like its men and women, are such as the Platonic Spenser loved to present, but not Plato. The 'divine Philosophy' had begun to 'charm' Milton long before; it had not yet pervaded his thought.

Doubtless the writer of *Comus* did not set himself to expound the doctrines of Plato, but, like poets from Homer to Yeats, simply used what in doctrine, as in image, legend, and myth, he found to his purpose. A great deal of what he found useful came originally from Plato, some of it directly; but genuine Platonism like the words to Diodati we can scarcely call it. The Platonism of *Comus* is still largely conventional because the author, though familiar with the Dialogues, and even partly under their sway, was not immediately concerned with them. What the letter to Diodati reveals was, then, not a new acquaintance with the Dialogues, but a new grasp of their bearing on Milton's own life.

Look again at the passage from the *Apology for Smectymnuus* quoted a few pages back. If Milton wrote thus, many years after *Comus* had been performed, clearly he did not feel that his Mask told what he had learned about chastity and love from the Dialogues. Far from it. Those 'divine volumes' have supplied him with matter for work yet unborn. And now, be it noted, the epithet 'divine' is no longer merely conventional, but granted by a disciple to the 'abstracted sublimities' into which he has himself been initiated. This is the language of an initiate, of one for whom the heart of an ethical doctrine has come alive. Knowing that Milton since his student days had been acquainted with Platonism, we recognize this experience of his 'riper years' as the winning of a new insight. The letter to Diodati, the postscript to the Elegies, the words in the *Apology*, all bear the mark of emotion, the two passages in prose, of strong emotion as well as clear understanding; they suggest, as it were, a philosophical conversion.

But we need not dwell on the emotional phase of Milton's Platonism. The bare references of his middle years alone warrant our finding in the Dialogues a major source of his theories on all the many problems of human life with which he then was dealing.

Thenceforth, at any rate, the authority of Plato assumed an ever-increasing importance. In the letter to Diodati, Milton had quoted from *Phaedrus* without giving his source; a year later he was more explicit. He wrote to Buommattei:

> It is Plato's opinion that an alteration in the style and fashion of dress portends grave disorders and changes in the State. (Tillyard, p. 16.)

That is Plato's opinion in the *Laws* (7. 797-8); the illustration of clothes is given only once, but in connection with a doctrine basic to the *Laws* as a whole, that unnecessary and careless change, like all instability, is at once a cause and sign of decay. Though it may seem strange for an advocate of divorce and regicide, Milton accepted the principle, applying it here to language as earnestly as Plato had applied it to dress. Indeed it became for Milton a constant guide, too little observed by readers of his prose, who naturally are more struck by its more striking corollary, that needed and deliberate corrections of evil signify and produce vitality.

And now, with Milton's entrance into the struggles of politics, his citations from Plato become more frequent. Their manner, too, changes; for controversial writing is of another sort than academic orations and verses, or even friendly letters, and demands from a writer a much clearer statement of the ground of his assertions. Schoolmasters and friends presumably know what we have read, and will accept allusive references; but opponents need to be con-

vinced. The reader of poetry does not wish to have footnotes thrust into the text; the reader of polemic writing
insists upon them. Whether or not this difference in the
type of Milton's writing was responsible, he seemingly
became a careful student of the Dialogues during the years
of England's civil war. In his various treatises, the allusions and citations are specific and detailed, so much so
that a scholar must still read the words of Plato as carefully as Milton did in order to find the exact source. But
even more striking than this exactness is the manifest wish
to grasp Plato's thought and hold it steadily in view. The
reference, while imbedded in argument, often has a bit
of commentary attached; that is, Milton comments not
merely on its relevance to the argument, but on the reason-
ableness of the position taken by Plato. Most important of
all, these citations of Plato as an authority show not understanding alone, but an incorporation of the thought into
Milton's own doctrine; they do not simply add the prop
of a great name to the argument, they guide it.

In his first political writing, *Of Reformation* (3. 39),
Milton cites for the organic conception of the State the
authority of Plato, Aristotle, and the Bible. The following
year, in the *Reason of Church-Government*, he gives Plato
more prominence, opening his treatise with these words:

> In the publishing of human laws, which for the most part aim
> not beyond the good of civil society, to set them barely forth
> to the people without reason or preface like a physical prescript,
> or only with threatenings as it were a lordly command, in the
> judgment of Plato was thought to be done neither generously nor
> wisely. (3. 181.)[9]

The advice of Plato is then given in detail, and confirmed
by the example of Moses. A little further in the Preface
(3. 182), Plato is called 'the wisest of the heathen.' Naturally Milton's interest in political theory led him to a care-

---

[9] Cf. Plato, *Laws* 4. 718 and elsewhere, and the Third *Epistle*.

ful study of the two great political theorists of antiquity; but since Plato, unlike Aristotle, presented his politics as an integrated part of his ethics, and indeed of his entire body of thought, Milton would consider works other than the *Republic* and *Laws* in order to grasp the meaning of Plato's doctrines on the State. It is, therefore, not strange to find in the *Reason of Church-Government* allusions to *Protagoras* and the *Sophist*. 'I read,' says Milton,

of no Sophister among the Greeks that was so dear, neither Hippias nor Protagoras, nor any whom the Socratic school famously refuted without hire. (3. 202.)

And later:

And he that will not let these [admonition and reproof] pass into him, though he be the greatest king, as Plato affirms, must be thought to remain impure within, and unknowing of those things wherein his pureness and his knowledge should most appear. (3. 264.)

Milton's very use of the term 'Sophist'—and he uses it with growing frequency and scorn in his controversial writings—apparently comes from his reading in the Dialogues, though the word was common in his time as now. At any rate, in his *Apology for Smectymnuus,* he again associates refutation of sophistry with the Socratic method, and elsewhere repeats the argument of Plato that those who deal in truth for hire cannot be true teachers.[10]

From the *Apology* we may cull further passages bearing on his Platonic studies:

This we know in Laertius, that the mimes of Sophron were of such reckoning with Plato as to take them nightly to read on and after make them his pillow. (3. 293.)[11]

---

[10] See *Apology for Smectymnuus* (3. 293-4), and cf. *Pro Se Defensio* (9. 284) and *The Means to Remove Hirelings* (6. 46).

[11] See Diogenes Laertius, *Life of Plato* 18; and cf. Olympiodorus, *Life of Plato*, and Athenaeus, *Deipnosophists* 11. 504 b.

If every book which may by chance excite to laugh here and there must be termed thus, then may the Dialogues of Plato, who for those his writings hath obtained the surname of Divine, be esteemed, as they are by that detractor in Athenaeus, no better than mimes. Because there is scarce one of them, especially wherein some notable Sophister lies sweating and turmoiling under the inevitable and merciless dilemmas of Socrates, but that he who reads, were it Saturn himself, would be often robbed of more than a smile. (3. 293-4.)[12]

That grave and noble invention which the greatest and sub-limest wits in sundry ages, Plato in *Critias,* and our own two famous countrymen, the one in his *Utopia,* the other in his *New Atlantis,* chose, I may not say as a field, but as a mighty continent wherein to display the largeness of their spirits by teaching this our world better and exacter things than were yet known or used. (3. 294.)

[I have] read of heathen philosophers some to have taught that whosoever would but use his ear to listen might hear the voice of his guiding Genius ever before him, calling and as it were pointing to that way which is his part to follow. (3. 318.)[13]

Milton has read Diogenes Laertius' *Life of Plato* and the discussions of Plato in Athenaeus' *Deipnosophists.* He is, then, familiar not only with the works of Plato, but with some writings about them. He has analyzed the method of Socratic refutation. He recognizes in *Critias* the pattern of More's *Utopia* and Bacon's *New Atlantis,* and here praises the Utopian fiction as a means of teaching—a point to remember when we come upon his criticism in *Areopagitica* of 'Atlantic and Utopian polities.'

Thus from the year 1637, at latest, until 1642, the So-cratic doctrine given in 'the divine volumes of Plato,' and

---

[12] See Athenaeus, *Deipnosophists* 11. 504 b-509 e, where Pontianus speaks scornfully of Plato's Dialogues, and 10. 440 b, where Plato is called ὁ Θειότατος.

[13] See Plato's *Apology* 27 and 31, *Symposium* 175 and 220, and especially *Phaedo* 107-8, 113. And cf. Xenophon, *Apology* 3-9, and *Memorabilia* 1.4.15-16; 4.3.12; and 4.8.1.

reinforced by the writings of Xenophon, represents an important element in Milton's thought; and not only the Socratic doctrine of love, though that itself is the whole ethical doctrine, as Milton explains:

> The first and chiefest office of love begins and ends in the soul, producing those happy twins of her divine generation, knowledge and virtue.

Moreover, he not only recognizes, but insists upon, the Platonic view that ethics is the inclusive study of moral theory for the individual, and political theory for the State. It is, indeed, because this is his own belief that Milton as poet and Milton as political writer are one, with the one consistent purpose of leading men through knowledge and virtue to happiness individual and communal.

Accordingly, if we ask to which realm of Milton's thought Platonic doctrine is the key, the answer must be to all of it, since for Milton as for Plato, the parts of life are not separate, but in organic unity; and what is now treated as the law of ecclesiastical organization is again the principle of writing poetry. We can distinguish only phases, not disjunct components, of his philosophy. But if Platonism helps to explain the entire range of Milton's views, it explains them only in part, or only as fused with other doctrines and modified by them. Of these, the most important is, of course, Christianity; the rest, with a man of such varied reading and high power of assimilation as Milton, can scarcely be analyzed here. Perhaps we must even hesitate to assign to Platonism the second highest power in forming Milton's mature thought. But the emphasis on Plato in the *Apology for Smectymnuus* confirms our view: Milton himself did not hesitate to assert a momentous debt to Plato, and besides the Bible, he pays to no other writings an equally high compliment.

The question to which part of Plato's writing he gave this praise must be answered as generally. In the Tractate

Of Education, he prescribes the 'moral works of Plato,' perhaps meaning the dialogues which Diogenes Laertius classified as 'ethical': the *Apology, Crito, Phaedo, Phaedrus,* the *Symposium, Menexenus, Clitophon,* the Epistles, *Philebus, Hipparchus,* and the *Rivals.* Perhaps he knew some of these to be spurious. But since he also wished to have the principles of rhetoric 'taught out of the rule of Plato,' he would add at least *Gorgias* to the list. His own references to Plato up through the publication of the *Apology for Smectymnuus* include specific citations of *Phaedrus,* the *Laws,* the *Sophist,* and *Critias,* with probable allusions to *Protagoras* and the *Symposium,* and general remarks on Plato that suggest a familiarity with all his writings. In later works,[14] he specifically mentions the *Symposium, Protagoras, Gorgias,* the *Republic,* and the Eighth *Epistle;* and he often alludes to the dialogues listed above. If we are to include the examples in his *Logic* among his own citations of Plato, other dialogues must be added: *Cratylus* and the *First Alcibiades, Philebus, Crito, Phaedo, Meno,* and the *Statesman.* There are, in addition, numerous places where he cites an opinion of Plato's without naming the dialogue or epistle in which it appears. We have every reason to think him familiar with all the writings commonly ascribed to Plato.

One further question remains: granted that Milton was deeply impressed by Platonic doctrine some time before 1642, how permanent was the impression? We may continue through his writings, no longer quoting every reference, but only those which suggest either continuity or a break in the Platonic influence. In the *Doctrine and Discipline of Divorce,* Diotima's myth of the birth of love is compared with the Mosaic account of the Garden of Eden (3. 398). Later in that treatise, Milton asks 'what would Plato have deemed' of England's inconsistent laws on marriage (3. 458-9), and associates with his own belief

---

[14] See the appended table, p. 22.

in the identity of good laws and the law of nature the 'high principles' of Socrates in *Gorgias* (3. 500-1).

Areopagitica is the one work in which Milton ever disparaged any writing of Plato; and even there Plato remains 'a man of high authority indeed,' though 'least of all for his Commonwealth, in the book of his *Laws*' (4. 316). Since Milton elsewhere often uses the authority of that very work to support his own arguments, we may suppose that not the *Laws* in its entirety, but only its advocacy of censorship roused his dissent; and many another Platonist has found it as hard to reconcile himself to some of the legal constraints Plato seemingly urged. But Milton, be it noted, ends his discussion of the censorship in the *Laws* by commending in its place another principle from the same work:

> Nor is it Plato's licensing of books will do this [that is, mend our condition], which necessarily pulls along with it so many other kinds of licensing; . . . but those unwritten or at least unconstraining laws of virtuous education, religious and civil nurture, which Plato there mentions as the bonds and ligaments of the Commonwealth, the pillars and the sustainers of every written statute, these they be which will bear chief sway in such matters as these. (4. 318.)

Plato naturally has a large part in the Tractate *Of Education,* not only among the books to be given to students, but in the theory and plan of instruction there set forth. And later works show how large a part the Dialogues had in Milton's self-education. In *Tetrachordon* he cites Plato three times; in the first *Defensio,* repeatedly turns to the *Laws* and Eighth *Epistle* to confirm his political theory; and in the *Defensio,* nine years after the *Apology for Smectymnuus,* reasserts his old judgment by naming Plato among the 'best and wisest men of old,' and once more calling him 'divine' (7. 349-51).

The Dialogues kept their hold upon Milton. Although the *Defensio Secunda, Pro Se Defensio,* and *Accidence*

Commenced Grammar have fewer references, the choice of Ramus' *Dialectica* as the basis for his *Logic* still shows a decided Platonic bent.[15] And finally the controversy between Satan and Jesus in *Paradise Regained* illuminates Milton's latest views on Plato. The first part of Athens to which Satan points in his last desperate attempt to win Jesus is

> the Olive Grove of Academe,
> Plato's retirement, where the Attic Bird
> Trills her thick-warbl'd notes the summer long. (4. 244-6.)

The first of the philosophers whose knowledge is offered are Socrates and his most illustrious pupil:

> To sage Philosophy next lend thine ear,
> From Heaven descended to the low-rooft house
> Of Socrates, see there his Tenement,
> Whom well inspir'd the Oracle pronounc'd
> Wisest of men; from whose mouth issu'd forth
> Mellifluous streams that water'd all the schools
> Of Academics old and new. (4. 272-8.)

Jesus had previously said:

> Poor Socrates (who next more memorable?)
> By what he taught and suffer'd for so doing,
> For truth's sake suffering death unjust, lives now
> Equal in fame to proudest Conquerours. (3. 96-9.)

But now he modifies Satan's compliment to Socrates:

> The first and wisest of them all profess'd
> To know this only, that he nothing knew. (4. 293-4.)[16]

Of Plato, all that Jesus says is

> The next to fabling fell and smooth conceits. (4. 295.)

---

[15] See Frank Pierrepont Graves, *Peter Ramus and the Educational Reformation of the Sixteenth Century.*

[16] Note that while Satan calls Socrates 'wisest of men,' Jesus calls him wisest only of the pagan philosophers.

Now since the other pagan philosophers are criticized in terms of their doctrine, Plato appears to come off easily in this stern rejection of all pagan learning. At any rate, next to Socrates, he is the Greek thinker least denounced. And Milton's words are not a very serious charge for a poet to bring against a philosopher; for if Plato 'fell' to 'fabling and smooth conceits,' his fall was from philosophy to poetry.

Milton did indeed think Plato poetical, recognizing in him the 'grave and noble' faculty of invention. He thought Plato a master of comic invention too (*Ap. Smect.* 3. 293-4; *Tetrach.* 4. 76), an authority on educational theory (*Of Ed.* 4. 287), a model of literary decorum (*Pro Se Def.* 9. 176), and an expert in law (*D.D.D.* 3. 458-9). In short he gave to Plato a position far above any other author, pagan or Christian, save the authors of the Bible. Never to Augustine, his favorite among Church-Fathers, to Spenser, his favorite among English poets, to Cicero, Erasmus, or Bacon, did he apply the epithet he granted to Plato. And far from merely adopting a conventional term of praise, he showed that he independently approved the common judgment, explaining that Plato 'for those his writings hath obtained the surname of Divine' (3. 293).

We can see that Milton was well-equipped by study to confirm and explain the ancient judgment. Note in the table of references how often he alludes to a specific passage in Plato, from how wide a range in the Dialogues and Epistles his allusions are drawn, and with what precision he refers to the *Laws* and Epistles, which are among the least generally read of Plato's works. If the references he took from Downham's commentary on Ramus should not be counted as his own, the choice at least is his, since he omitted innumerable others in condensing the commentary. And two changes he made suggest that what he took unchanged, he took with full knowledge of the works alluded to. Once, where Downham had omitted the specific source, Milton supplied *Phaedrus;*[17] and again, to Downham's illustrative phrase, *'philosophus pro Aristotele,'* Milton significantly added *'aut Platone.'*[18]

The two amendments confirm Milton's thorough knowledge of and enthusiastic admiration for Plato. What that knowledge and enthusiasm meant in his own thought and writing as yet has hardly been probed. For put *Paradise Lost* and *Paradise Regained* to the same test as we earlier put *Comus,* and we get a different result. Suppose Plato were dealing with the loss of human happiness, would he give the same explanation as Milton in the tale of man's fall? On the whole, we may say yes. True, he would conceive of no such perfect Providence watching—and waiting to relieve—mankind's errors. And Plato, to be sure, never plumbed so deep in Hell as Milton. Doubtless the Hebraic view of life brings to its disciples greater struggles as well as greater aspirations than Hellenism at its best. But if we look aside from Hell and Heaven to Earth, where Milton after all wished us most steadily to fix our gaze, and discern in the struggle there the meaning it had for Milton, we see that, however little the words and acts resemble those of a Platonic dialogue, the underlying argument is largely that of Plato. And when we turn to *Paradise Regained,* where a bolder Sophist than any opponent of Socrates defies a more glorious seeker after truth, even if the very dialectical method by which Jesus wins his victory did not point to the Dialogues as a model, the themes and arguments show how much Milton had assimilated from Plato.

---

[17] See in the appended table the note to the reference *Logic*, C. E. II. * 22.

[18] See the note to *Logic*, C. E. II. ** 334.

A TABLE OF MILTON'S REFERENCES TO SOCRATES AND PLATO[1]

	Passage	Date	Source	Quoted
S	*Eleg.* 4. 23-4	1627	? I *Alcib.*, 103 ff., 135	Agar 15
P	*Idea Plat.*	1628 or later	*passim;* esp. ?*Phaedo,* ?*Phaedr.,* ?*Sym.,* ?*Rep.*	Agar 16
P	*Prolus.* 2, C. E. 12. 150	1625-9	?*Rep.* 10. 616-7	Agar 76
	Prolus. 6, C. E. 12	1625-9		
S	*218		?*Apol.* 20-3[2]	
S	*238		*passim*	
	Prolus. 7, C. E. 12	1625-9		
P	262-4			Agar 77
S	*280		*passim*	
P	*Il Pen.* 87-96	1631-4	?*Tim.* 41-2	Agar 5
[P]	To Dio., C. E. 12. 26	1637	*Phaedr.*	Agar 72
P	To Buom., C. E. 12. 32	1638	*Laws* 7. 797-8	Agar 73
P	*Of Ref.,* C. E. 3. 39	1641	?*Rep.,* esp. 4. 420; ?*Laws,* esp. 5. 739	Agar 53
S	*Animad.*, C. E. 3. 161	1641	(Xenophon)[3]	

---

[1] The symbols used in the table are as follows:

S and *P* indicate references to Socrates and Plato. Parentheses are used to distinguish implicit references, as in the letter to Diodati, where Milton quotes *Phaedrus,* but does not name his source.

The single asterisk marks a reference not given in Agar's *Milton and Plato.* The double asterisk marks a reference given neither in the Columbia Index nor by Agar.

C.E. with Arabic numbers following refers to the Columbia edition of *The Works of John Milton,* volume and page. The numbers in parentheses correspond to Milton's own divisions.

A question mark before a title indicates uncertainty in assigning the allusion to any specific work of Plato.

The number after *Agar* refers to the passage in the Appendix of Agar's volume where the selection is quoted.

The page-number under *Downham* marks the place in the work of George Downham, *Rami Dialecticae Libri Duo cum Commentariis* (London, 1669), which is the source of Milton's reference. Milton, of course, used an earlier edition of Downham's commentary.

The list does not include those passages in the *Logic* where Socrates is named merely as a convenient Everyman of argument.

[2] The most likely source is Diogenes Laertius, *Life of Socrates,* 36-8. See also Xenophon's *Banquet* 2. 10. Diogenes Laertius seems to take the statement of the oracle from Plato's *Apology* and the character of Xanthippe from Xenophon.

[3] This is the sole reference to Socrates in which Milton uses Xenophon alone as the authority. See Xenophon, *Apology* 26; *Memorabilia* 1. 2. 1-8; 1. 6. 11-3.

	Passage	Date	Source	Quoted
	Church-Gov., C. E. 3	1642		
P	*181-2 (Preface)		*Laws* 4. 718 ff.	
S	*202 (1. 5)		*passim*; esp. *Protag.*, ?*Hipp. Min.*	
P	264 (2. 3)		*Soph.* 230; ?*Gorg.* 476 ff.	Agar 54
	Ap. Smect., C. E. 3	1642		
PS	293-4		*passim*[4]	Agar 55
P	*294		*Critias*	
P	305		*passim*; esp. *Phaedr.*, *Sym.*	Agar 57
	D.D.D., C. E. 3	1643		
PS	398 (1. 4)		*Sym.* 203	Agar 58
P	441 (2. 3)		*passim*; esp. ?*Laws* 1. 644-5; ?*Meno 99-100*	Agar 60
P	*458-9 (2. 9)		*Laws* 4. 719	
P	464 (2. 11)		*Protag.* 354 e, 355-8; et al. Cf. *Meno* 77-8, *Tim.* 86	Agar 61
SP	500-1 (2. 21)		*Gorg.* 482-4, 488-510	Agar 62
	Judg. Bucer, C. E. 4	1644		
P	*24 (17 on Matth. v. 19)		(Bucer)[5] ?*Rep.*, ?*Laws*	
	Areop., C. E. 4	1644		
P	299			Agar 44
P	316		*Rep.*, *Laws*	Agar 46
P	317		*Rep.* 3; *Laws* 2, 7	Agar 47
P	318		*Rep.* 4; *Laws* 1, 7	Agar 48
	Of Ed., C. E. 4	1644		
S	281			Agar 66
P	284		*passim*	Agar 67
P	286		*passim*; esp. *Phaedr.*, *Gorg.*	Agar 68
P	287		*passim* and *Laws* 1. 634-5	Agar 69
[P]S	*Eleg.* 7, Postscript	before 1645	*passim*; esp. *Phaedr.*, *Sym.*	Agar 14
	Tetrach., C. E. 4	1645		
S	*70 (To Parl.)		?*Apol.* 19	
P	*76 (on Gen. i. 27)		*Sym.* 189-93	
P	81 (on Gen. i. 28)		*Laws* 6. 773-6, 783-5	Agar 63

[4] The first part of the reference comes from Diogenes Laertius, *Life of Plato* 18; the second from Milton's own reading of the Dialogues. 'That detractor in Athenaeus' is probably Pontianus in *Deipnosophists* 2. 504 b-509 e.

[5] Apparently taken from Martin Bucer, *Of the Kingdom of Christ*, Chap. 17.

Passage	Date	Source	Quoted
P *157-8 (on Matth. xix. 7-8)		*Rep.*	
Def., C. E. 7	1651		
P *158 (3)		*Rep.* 5. 463. Cf. *Laws* 4. 715	
P 166-8 (3)		*Laws* 4. 715; VIII *Epist.* 354	Agar 40
P 304 (5)		VIII *Epist.* 355	Agar 41
P *348-50 (6)		VIII *Epist.* 354-5	
S *Def. Sec.*, C. E. 8 192	1654	?*Apol.* 20-3	
Pro Se Def., C. E. 9	1655		
S *52		?*Apol.*	
S[P] *112		*passim*	
PS *176		*passim*	
P *180-2			
P *P. L.* 3. 471-3	before 1667		Agar 18
Grammar, C. E. 6	1669		
P **329 (2. Of the Concords)			
SP **349 (2. Of the Conjunctions)			
Logic, C. E. 11	1670		Downham
P *10 (Preface)		*Theaet.* 202 e	Proleg., p. 19
P **12 (Preface)		*Gorg.* 448	Proleg., p. 22
P *18-20 (1.1)		*Crat.*, I *Alcib.* 129 c	pp. 3-4
P *22 (1.2)		*Phaedr.* 235-6, 264	p. 15[6]
PS *58 (1.7)		*passim* (and Diogenes Laertius)	p. 79
P *66 (1.8)		*Phil.* 54	p. 88
P *96 (1.11)		*Rep.* 3. 405[7]	p. 122

[6] Milton gives the source as *Phaedrus* where Downham had simply said, '*Atque hanc distributionem Plato videtur primus attigisse.*'

[7] Milton's translator in the Columbia edition, Allan H. Gilbert, here makes a serious mistake. Quoting Downham, Milton writes: '*Hoc argumento Plato miseras civitates auguratur, quae medicorum et judicum multitudine indigeant, quia multum quoque et intemperantiam et injustitiam in ea civitate versari necesse est.*' The translation given is: 'By means of this argument Plato conjectures that "those states are wretched which lack a multitude of physicians and judges, since necessarily much intemperance and injustice will be practised in such a state." ' Clearly Plato says the very opposite in the *Republic* 3. 405, and Milton's '*multitudine indigeant*' must mean 'need a multitude.'

	Passage	Date	Source	Quoted
S [P]	*140-2 (1.16)		*Crito* 44	p. 164
P	*150 (1.18)			p. 177
S	*166 (1.18)			
P	*200 (1.21)		*Laws* 3, *Phaedo* 92	p. 209
S	*204 (1.21)			p. 212
S	*228 (1.25)		(Aristotle)	p. 242
P	*228-30 (1.25)		?*Phil.* 16-8,	pp. 243-4
			?*Statesm.* 287	
P	*238 (1.27)		*passim* and *Meno*	
			72-7.	pp. 249-50
P	*240 (1.27)		*Statesm.*	p. 251
P	*286 (1.33)		*Rep.* 5. 473	p. 290
P	*308 (2.3)		*Crat.* ?431	p. 324
P	**334 (2.4)			p. 365[8]
P	*470 (2.17)		*Phil.* 16	p. 472
P	*474 (2.17)		?*Phaedr.*, ?*Statesm.*	p. 428
P	**494 (Praxis)		?*Tim.*	p. 47
P.R.		1671		
S	3.96-9		*passim;* esp. ?*Apol.*	Agar 35
			29-31, 36-42;	
			?*Crito*, ?*Phaedo*	
P	4.244-7			Agar 37
S[P]	*4.272-8		?*Apol.* 20-3	
SP	4.293-5		*passim*	Agar 38
?*On Worthy Master*		?		
Shakespeare, C. E. 18. 361				
P	**15-8		*Tim.* 39	

---

[8] Downham had written, '*ut Poeta pro Homero aut Virgilio: philosophus pro Aristotele: orator pro Demosthene aut Cicerone.*' Milton inserts Plato as one for whom *philosophus* may stand: '*ut poeta pro Homero aut Virgilio, Philosophus pro Aristotele aut Platone et similia.*'

CHAPTER II

'Academics Old and New'

B Y THE SEVENTEENTH CENTURY the influence of Plato had so permeated European thought that few books Milton knew or might have known were untouched by it. The Bible itself, that rock on which he built his life, owes something to the Academy, if, as scholars tell us, the 'Logos' of St. John and St. Paul's doctrine of love have Platonic origins. At any rate, apart from the Bible, European literature can show little that owes no debt to Plato. Without writing the history of Platonism or noting every author in whose work Milton was likely to meet it, we may try to place him in the Platonic tradition. The seventeenth century continued the interest in Plato that the Florentine Academy had revived. Milton, abreast of his time, shared its best enthusiasms; and the zealous study of Plato that marked his age, his country, and his university, provided at least one channel through which the ancient philosophy reached him.

But Milton knew the tradition independently. He evidently studied ancient writers who throw light on the origins and development of Plato's doctrines, and he shows a marked preference for those who were closest to Platonic thought. For example, take the lists of reading commended in his Tractate *Of Education*. The most important of these is for the course in ethics, since the aim of the whole program is ethical and religious:

The end, then, of learning is to repair the ruins of our first parents by regaining to know God aright, and out of that knowledge to love Him, to imitate Him, to be like Him, as we may the nearest by possessing our souls of true virtue, which, being united to the heavenly grace of faith, makes up the highest perfection. (Ainsworth, p. 52.)

And again:

I call therefore a complete and generous education that which fits a man to perform justly, skilfully, and magnanimously all the offices, both private and public, of peace and war. (*Ibid.*, p. 55.)

Now the course in ethics is to be divided into two parts; first:

To season them and win them early to the love of virtue and true labor . . . some easy and delightful book of education would be read to them; whereof the Greeks have store, as Cebes, Plutarch, and other Socratic discourses. (*Ibid.*, p. 56.)

And later:

By this time, years and good general precepts will have furnished them more distinctly with that act of reason which in ethics is called *proairesis;* that they may with some judgment contemplate upon moral good and evil. Then will be required a special reinforcement of constant and sound indoctrinating to set them right and firm, instructing them more amply in the knowledge of virtue and the hatred of vice; while their young and pliant affections are led through all the moral works of Plato, Xenophon, Cicero, Plutarch, Laertius, and those Locrian remnants; but still to be reduced in their nightward studies wherewith they close the day's work, under the determinate sentence of David or Solomon, or the Evangels and Apostolic Scriptures. (*Ibid.*, p. 58.)

This avowed preference for 'Socratic discourses' on education together with the almost exclusively Platonic list of 'moral works' is highly significant in a writer of Milton's studied effects. And apparently he prescribes what was, at least in part, his own teaching practice; for according to Edward Phillips, his pupils read 'Plutarch's *Placita Philosophorum* and Περι Παιδων 'Αγογιας [*sic*].' (See Helen Darbishire's edition of the *Early Lives of Milton*, p. 60.) What light does all this throw on his Platonism?

First, Socrates was for Milton, even more than for many readers of Plato, a figure of unusual interest. From the early Fourth *Elegy* he remains a model of excellence even till *Paradise Regained*, where Jesus praises him as 'next memorable' to Job. All the extant writings of the Socratics won Milton's interest, the fragment of Aeschines (referred to in C.E. 11. 166) as well as Cebes' *Pinax* and the works of Xenophon and Plato. But it is to Xenophon next after Plato that a student of Socrates must turn.

According to Professor Saurat (*La Pensée de Milton*, p. 274), Milton was as much interested in the Socrates of Xenophon as in the Socrates of Plato. Professor Saurat refers us to the *Commonplace Book* for proof; but since neither Socrates nor Plato nor Xenophon appears in the *Commonplace Book*, we must suppose him to mean the *Accidence Commenced Grammar*, where Plato and Xenophon are linked as contemporaries (6. 329), and again as disciples of Socrates (6. 349). Actually there is only one point on which Milton uses Xenophon as a separate authority on Socrates. We are told in *Animadversions* (3. 161):

The heathen Philosophers thought that virtue was for its own sake inestimable, and the greatest gain of a teacher to make a soul virtuous; so Xenophon writes of Socrates, who never bargained with any for teaching him.[1]

The opinion Milton held on the relation of the three is best shown in a passage in his *Logic*, where he condenses

---

[1] See Xenophon's *Apology* 26 and *Memorabilia* 1. 2. 1-8; 1. 6. 11-13.

George Downham's commentary on the logical works of Peter Ramus. Now usually he kept very close to his original; but here Downham had written:

Doctrina Platonis et doctrina Socratis non possunt in quantitate comparari, nisi prius constet doctrinam utrique adjungi. (P. 289.)

Milton makes one change in the illustration: for Socrates he substitutes Xenophon:

Platonis doctrina et Xenophantis ante adjuncta utrique erat, quam comparata. (11. 150.)

It is a proper change. We have little certain knowledge of the doctrine of Socrates himself; what we know is the writings of two of his pupils. To what conclusions the comparison of Plato and Xenophon led Milton, his references show: Socrates appears in his pages as the figure Plato made the most interesting in the Dialogues.[2] And Xenophon is often merely an emphatic line drawn under Plato.

But Milton often associates Plato with others besides Socrates; with Pythagoras for example. Thus in the Tractate:

The course of study hitherto briefly described is, what I can guess by reading, likest to those ancient and famous schools of

---

[2] Thus the testimony of the oracle as Milton gives it in the Sixth *Prolusion* and *Paradise Regained* corresponds with Plato's *Apology* 21 rather than Xenophon's *Apology* 14. See also Milton's *Def. Sec.* (8. 192). With the reference to Socrates' profession of ignorance in the Seventh *Prolusion* (12. 280) compare especially Plato's *Apology* 21-3. The accusation of Socrates as given in *Tetrachordon* (4. 70) agrees with Plato's *Apology* 18. The refutation of sophists mentioned in the *Reason of Church-Government* (3. 202) as an activity of the 'Socratic school' suggests Plato rather than Xenophon. Similarly Milton's other allusions to Socrates, in *Pro Se Def.* (9. 176), *Ap. Smect.* (3.293, 318), and *Def. Sec.* (8. 74), all suggest the account of Plato rather than that of Xenophon.

Only one reference (in the Sixth *Prolusion* 12. 218) suggests a source in Xenophon (*Banquet* 2. 10) or Diogenes Laertius (2. 36-8).

Pythagoras, Plato, Isocrates, Aristotle, and such others. (Ainsworth, p. 61.)

The 'school of Pythagoras' is mentioned again in *Areopagitica* (4. 393), and with like respect. In the early Prolusion *De Sphaerarum Concentu* (12. 150) Aristotle is *'Pythagorae et Platonis aemulus et perpetuus Calumniator,'* while Plato wisely followed Pythagoras, *'Deum illum Philosophorum,'* in affirming the harmony of the spheres. May we not explain this enthusiasm for Pythagoras less by the fragmentary remains of Pythagorean writings than by Plato's debt to the school? Diogenes Laertius and Cicero had stressed the Pythagorean cast of Plato's thought.[3] Milton would be aware of it, and the respect he invariably pays to the 'Samian master' shows one basis for his sympathy with Platonism.

Most pre-Socratic thought apparently seemed to him, as to Plato, insignificant until joined with Pythagorean and Socratic teachings, for he shows no interest in it.[4] He does esteem the early Greek law-givers to the point of including them in his program of education,[5] and thus indicates sympathy with still another formative element in the thought of Plato.

The importance and respect accorded to Plato's various teachers reappears in the treatment Milton accords those who drew from Plato. He puts the 'Locrian remnants,' that is, the treatise *On the Soul of the World,* on the reading

---

[3] See Diogenes, *Life of Plato* 8; and Cicero, De Finibus 5. 87; *Tusculan Disputations* 1. 32; and *De Republica* 1. 10.

[4] Thus Milton's Jesus agrees with Satan that Socrates was the first pagan philosopher. See *P.R.* 4. 272-7, 293-4. A single reference to Protagoras occurs in *Areopagitica* (4. 299); otherwise Milton does not mention the pre-Socratic philosophers.

[5] *Of Ed.* (4. 285). Cf. *Republic* 10. 599 and *Timaeus* 20. For other references to Lycurgus and Solon in Plato, see *Phaedrus* 258, 278, and *Symposium* 209.

list of his academy and similarly commends Plutarch, Cicero, and 'Longinus.' Cicero especially was a favorite. From the early letters and *Prolusions* through the *Logic,* he is a constant authority, familiarly alluded to and quoted. And while his importance in the schools may in part account for the familiarity, the tone of these citations can be explained only by basic agreement. Milton explicitly calls him 'Academic' (11.138), cites a quotation of his from Plato (11.286), and frequently adds his words to support Platonic theory.[6] He appears with Plato again in the Tractate among authorities on rhetoric. Indeed it is a highly Platonic rhetoric that Milton wished to have taught 'out of the rule of Plato, Aristotle, Phalereus, Cicero, Hermogenes, Longinus' (Ainsworth, pp. 59-60). The list begins with Plato, whose treatment of the art is singularly unlike that of the usual rhetorician; it includes, besides Cicero, who tried to reconcile rhetoric with the doctrines of the Academy, the essay of Demetrius of Phalerum with its many quotations from Plato and frequent praise of his style; and it ends with the treatise that, more than any other work on the subject, applies to the art of persuasion the spirit and canons of Plato's teaching. The epistle of 'Longinus' *On the Sublime* might stand as a Platonic discourse on rhetoric. Cicero, we may think, lent Milton support for the view that rhetoric may be taught out of 'the rule of Plato,' and 'Longinus' confirmed him in it.

Taken as a whole, the lists in the Tractate suggest that Milton's view of education was 'Socratic,' his concept of rhetoric largely 'Academic,' and his ethical theory almost entirely Platonic. He evidently was aware of what he omitted from the course in ethics, for having named only Socratic and Platonic authors, he concludes with the reminder that these are still to be supplemented with the 'de-

---

[6] See, for example, *Logic* (11.22); *D.D.D.* (3.441); *Tetrach.* (4.157-8); *Def.* (7.166-8, 304-6).

terminate sentence' of Holy Scripture. Diogenes Laertius, to be sure, would present varieties of ethical opinion; yet even he emphasizes rather than moderates the Academic bias of the 'moral works' to be taught; for Diogenes gave Platonism preferential treatment. (See especially the *Lives* 3. 47.) Despite the inclusion, then, of the *Lives and Opinions of Eminent Philosophers,* the question remains: Why did Milton not allow Epicurean, Stoic, and, most important, Peripatetic, to speak for themselves? With Stoic and Epicurean, the answer is surely that Milton cared little for what they might say. He invariably refers to Epicureanism and Stoicism with contempt; and though he respects Lucretius, Seneca, and Chrysippus, it is not for the distinctly Epicurean or Stoic parts of their moral teaching. But the same explanation will not hold for the silence imposed on Aristotle. Clearly, in order to place Milton in the Platonic tradition we must understand his opinion of Plato's first great pupil.

On the whole, he thought decidedly well of 'Aristotle, our chief instructor in the universities' (6. 136), and turned to his authority early and late. Once while still at Cambridge, he took issue with his 'chief instructor' for disagreeing with Pythagoras and Plato on the music of the spheres, and called him their *'aemulus et perpetuus Calumniator'* (12. 150), just as later he made sport of the Aristotelian misreading of the Platonic Idea. These disparaging remarks both involve a comparison favoring Plato. Otherwise Aristotle is usually treated with respect, even in *De Doctrina Christiana* where Milton makes some effort to disentangle the interwoven threads of Aristotelian and scholastic theology. (See especially 14. 48; 15. 8.) Again in his *Logic,* following Downham and Ramus, Milton often cites Aristotle as evidence and authority. More important, the Aristotelian *Poetics,* which in the Tractate *Of Education* Milton placed first among the readings on 'that sublime

33

art,' is a basis for the prefatory note to *Samson Agonistes*.

We may conclude that Milton did not underestimate Aristotle, and recognized him as one of 'the best interpreters of nature and morality,' but none the less rejected the Aristotelian way of thought. Why, we learn from a passage in the *Doctrine and Discipline of Divorce*. Here Milton deals with an apparent disagreement between Plato and Aristotle, not jestingly as in the Second *Prolusion* and the verses *De Idea Platonica*, but seriously. He writes:

> It is the constant opinion of Plato in *Protagoras* and other of his dialogues, agreeing with that proverbial sentence among the Greeks, that 'no man is wicked willingly'—which also the Peripatetics do rather distinguish than deny. (3. 464. Cf. *Nicomachean Ethics* 7. 1-10.)

Milton recognized what many students forget, that Plato taught Aristotle for long years to the apparent satisfaction of both, and that the writings of master and pupil disagree far less than those of the militant Platonists and Aristotelians of later generations. On Milton's page, the two often appear together in support of the same doctrine, and their agreement is not forced. The emphasis is right; in general, Aristotle does 'rather distinguish than deny' Platonic teachings. And where Aristotle 'distinguished,' Milton often accepted the refinement.

But where he denied, Milton was cautious. In ethics Aristotle denied too often, at any rate, denied the most important point; and hence the omission in the Tractate and the contempt shown for his moral system in *Paradise Regained* 4. 297-8:

> Others in virtue plac'd felicity,
> But virtue join'd with riches and long life.

These are, of course, the Peripatetics; and the doctrine condemned is central to their ethical system.

Among the ancients, then, Milton gave special attention

to those who present elements of the Platonic philosophy—
Socratics, ancient law-givers, Pythagoreans—and those who
show his pervasive influence—Cicero, Plutarch, 'Longinus.'
How did he regard the Neoplatonists whom his contemporaries revered as true interpreters of the Platonic tradition?
We have seen in Chapter 1 that he associated Hermes
Trismegistus with Plato both in the verses *De Idea Platonica* and in *Il Penseroso*. He may even have accepted the
philosophical genealogy sanctioned by Ficino:

> Eo tempore quo Moyses natus est, floruit Athlas . . . ; cuius
> nepos fuit Mercurius Trismegistus. . . . Primus igitur theologiae
> appellatus est auctor. Eum secutus Orpheus, . . . Aglaophamus,
> . . . Picthagoras, . . . Philolaus . . . Divi Platonis nostri praecep-
> tor. Itaque una priscae theologiae undique sibi consona secta ex
> theologis sex miro quodam ordine conflata est, exordia sumens a
> Mercurio, a Divo Platone peritus absoluta. (See *Hermetica*, ed.
> and trans. by Scott, 1.31.)

Perhaps, as Agar observes, Milton later came to see how
foreign the *Hermetica* is to the true Platonic spirit, and yet
something of Hermetic mysticism remains even in *Paradise
Lost*. The demonology which *Il Penseroso* associates with
Hermes (rightly) and Plato (wrongly) reappears not only
in the 'attendant Spirit' of *Comus* ('daemon' in the manuscript), the 'Genius of the shore' in *Lycidas* 183, and the
'*Angelus unicuique suus*' of the first poem *Ad Leonoram*,
but at the end of the sonnet on his blindness and even in
Paradise Lost 4.677-8:

> Millions of spiritual Creatures walk the Earth
> Unseen, both when we wake, and when we sleep.

These are the Hermetic

> Daemons that are found
> In fire, air, flood, or under ground,
> Whose power hath a true consent
> With Planet, or with Element. (*Il Penseroso* 93-6.)

35

Probably Milton, like his contemporaries, knew the work of Michael Psellus in Ficino's translation, *De Daemonibus,* and other similar writings. C. S. Lewis has shown in *A Preface to Paradise Lost* (pp. 105-11) how largely the 'Platonic' theories then current explain Milton's angels.

But the age studied more sober Platonists as well, the Neoplatonists, pagan, Jewish, and Christian, who had kept something, if not the whole, of Plato's doctrines alive in Europe during the centuries when little more than *Timaeus* was known. (See A. E. Taylor, *A Commentary on Plato's Timaeus,* pp. 2-3.) To scholars of the Renaissance, newly familiar with Plato but long familiar with the Neoplatonists, they seemed valid interpreters of Plato's thought. Plotinus especially was to influence the general understanding of Plato; for Ficino, who set the style in Platonism, translated and commented on the *Enneads* as a proper sequel to the Dialogues. And hence Coleridge jests that the Cambridge Platonists should rather be called 'Plotinists.' Like Dr. Whichcote, who 'set young students much on reading the ancient philosophers, chiefly Plato, Tully, Plotin,' Henry More, chief of the Cambridge group, studied the 'Platonic writers, Marsilius Ficinus, Plotinus himself, Mercurius Trismegistus, and the mystical divines.' John Tulloch, in *Rational Theology . . . in the Seventeenth Century,* speaks thus of the Cambridge Platonists:

> They betray no suspicion of the enormous interval of thought betwixt Plato and Plotinus, still less of any growth or development of thought in Plato himself. . . . Plotinus is the chief favorite. . . . The suspicion that Plotinus and Proclus, while building upon the Platonic basis, may have had little or none of the spirit of the master-builder, never disturbed them. (2.479-81.)

The judgment here expressed is rather harsh. Let us say rather that the age was more concerned with the mystical part of Plato—and surely we must grant that Plato is partly mystic—as developed and magnified by Plotinus and his .students, than with the severely rational part which we often consider the whole of Platonism. We need not, however, stay longer with Plotinus and his disciples; for Milton, in a period which thought the *Enneads* the very echo of Plato, pays almost no attention to pagan Neoplatonists. His few references to Porphyry and Proclus indicate little admiration for their views, and Plotinus he does not even mention.

At the same time, however little interest he may have expressed in Plotinus, Milton had much in common with the Cambridge group. In a study of the *Platonic Tradition in Anglo-Saxon Philosophy* (pp. 29-31), Muirhead lists among their major doctrines: (1) the belief that Heaven and Hell are states of soul rather than places; (2) the identification of Reason with God; (3) an insistence that true freedom dwells only in reason and in the control of life by reason; and (4) the conviction that faith and reason, far from being at odds, are fundamentally alike, and lead to the same persuasions. We recognize these as views held by Milton. Parallels between the Cambridge Platonists and Milton have been demonstrated by Elbert N. S. Thompson,[7] Marjorie H. Nicolson,[8] and Ernst Cassirer;[9] and further investigations are sure to reveal other similarities, for there is much in Milton's writing that cannot be called by any name but Neoplatonism.

A closer tie between Milton and contemporary Platonists may be their common interest in the writers who first attempted to reconcile Plato with Holy Writ; Philo Judaeus, for example, who began the system of Biblical exegesis which made of the text a peg from which to suspend Plato's

---

[7] See 'A Forerunner of Milton,' *MLN.* 32 (1917). 479-82.
[8] 'The Spirit World of Milton and More,' *SP.* 22 (1925). 433-52.
[9] *Die Platonische Renaissance in England*, p. 23.

37

doctrines.[10] Milton took Philo as an authority, or at least recognized his repute with the age, for he justifies an argument in his first *Defensio* thus:

Another solid authority, Josephus' contemporary Philo Judaeus, one very studious in the law of Moses, upon the whole of which he wrote an extensive commentary, when in his book concerning the creation of the king he interprets this chapter of the law, releases the king from the law no otherwise than as an enemy may be said to be so released. (7. 78-9.)

He goes on to quote a few words in Greek, and then continues with a Latin translation of the passage. Evidently he knew Philo well.

Far more important to him was Augustine, in whose work Platonic thought, already adapted to Christianity by Clement and Origen, became its very handmaid. With Protestants Augustine was especially popular; he presented a doctrine convenient to oppose to the Thomism dominant in the Roman Church, just as the Platonic theories upon which he had based his doctrine were a useful answer to the Aristotelian theories on which Thomas had built. With Protestant Milton he was a favorite, the most often quoted and consistently respected of the Churchmen. And Augustine's Christian Platonism is doubtless the chief link between Milton and other Platonists of the time, especially the group at Cambridge. Here is much the same union as they and Milton make between Platonic and Biblical precept, the conversion of Platonic ethics and cosmology to the divine order of the universe, the identification of the radiant Idea of the Good with the unapproachable light of God, the interpretation of every major Christian doctrine—save the most important, that of the Man Divine—in the terms of Platonism and Neoplatonism. Augustine's scale of being, or the successive emanations which descend like a ladder

---

[10] See, for example, Philo, *Special Laws* i. 327-9.

from God, is Neoplatonic, though it derives from the Dialogues. Similarly the constant figure of God as light, of truth as illumination, comes through Plotinus, and perhaps Manicheism, though ultimately from the Allegory of the Cave in the *Republic*. But the emphasis on these doctrines in Augustine and the later Church is assuredly closer to the spirit of Plotinus than to Plato.

Here, then, in the Christian use of Neoplatonism, rather than in the works of Plotinus, Porphyry, and Proclus themselves, we may find the source of Milton's Neoplatonic-sounding phrases on light (*e.g.*, *P.L.* 3. 1-6) and the scale of being (*P.L.* 5. 469-79).

Augustine and such Augustinian scholastics as Scotus Erigena also help to explain Milton's use of the cosmological and eschatological myths of Plato, although they took the myths from Neoplatonists and he directly from Plato. The ordering of the world out of elementary chaos, the figure of God as father of the created universe, of formless space as the mother, the institution of the dance-like planetary changes to serve man's reckoning of time and draw his mind by contemplation to the worship of their maker; all these cosmological theories from Plato's *Timaeus* constantly recur in Milton's writing, though either barely suggested in the Bible or totally foreign to it. Their use, justified by the precedent of Christian Neoplatonists, serves to expand the poetic brevity of the Bible. Even when Milton speaks of the soul's native star (as in *Damon* 123) Christian tradition gives him warrant. Dante too used this Platonic myth, and long before Dante it had become a part of Christian lore.

So also with the accounts of the after-life in *Phaedo, Gorgias,* and the *Republic*. References to Hell and Heaven are few and brief in the Bible, and no mention at all of Purgatory is to be found there. In Protestant fashion Milton has no Purgatory in the hereafter, but for the rest

39

adopts Plato's myths to supplement Scripture. Again, Christian precedent is behind him, and the habit of Christian Platonists in the age is with him. Even when he slips on a very few occasions into suggesting that the soul enjoyed a previous existence, as in *Ad Patrem* 30-1, the Christian mysticism of the time supports him.

On all these counts it seems reasonable to modify Agar's conclusions about the relation of Milton to traditional Platonism. Milton, says Agar,

the first in Europe so far as I have discovered, read and studied Plato with a mind freed from the influence of the Alexandrians and their Renaissance disciples, and so attained to an understanding of the dialogues. (P. 31.)

We recognize the change that Agar marks from the kind of Platonic material Milton used in his earlier poems to the kind he used in his prose and later poetry. In *Comus* Milton was still dealing chiefly with the supra-terrestrial doctrines of the Neoplatonists. These remain in *Paradise Lost;* but here, and yet more in *Paradise Regained* and *Samson Agonistes,* the more strictly ethical parts of Plato assume a major importance, while demonology and accounts of the creation are subordinated to the primary questions of human happiness. Yet this change in Platonic materials does not distinguish Milton's from all other Platonism of the age. Apart from the group at Cambridge, there were many who studied Plato; and some among them surely pentrated to his meaning. His main doctrines are not hard to grasp; to say they are is to charge Plato with an obscurity of which he is not guilty.[11]

---

[11] One example may suffice. In his *Discourse on the Light of Nature* 6 (quoted by E. T. Campagnac in *The Cambridge Platonists*, pp. 245-7), Nathanael Culverwel takes right reason as the natural law graven in the heart of man, and cites the argument in Plato's *Gorgias* to support his view in very much the same way as Milton does in *D.D.D.* (3. 458, 500-1) and *Eikon.* (5. 121).

It is Agar's view that, in passages like *Paradise Lost* 12. 82-104,

Milton takes a number of Plato's fundamental conceptions, such as the identity of virtue and reason, the tripartite division of the soul, the analogy between the soul and the State, and uses them to explain the condition of man. These ideas did not come from Spenser, or Ficino, or Margaret of Navarre. They are foreign to the spirit of Renaissance Platonism, and represent an aspect of the philsopher to which that period was indifferent. (P. 31.)

The statement is only partly true: these Platonic doctrines are not peculiar to Milton.[12] Nor was the spirit of Renaissance Platonism foreign to him.

To be sure, we find no references to the Florentine Academy in Milton's writing, except for one passing allusion to Bembo (3. 236). But Milton doubtless knew something of its work. Probably he used Ficino's translation of Plato, if not his commentaries. And in his visit to Italy, he may have heard talk at the various academies about their Florentine model. While in Florence, he wrote to Benedetto Buommattei, asking,

who among all the host of authors can justly claim the second place after the acknowledged masters of the Florentine tongue, who excels in tragedy, who writes lively and elegant comedy, who shows acuteness or depth of thought in letters or dialogues, and who has a noble style in historical writing. (Tillyard, p. 18.)

Some Florentine Platonists would be named in such a list, and would again be among the writers whose works Milton had shipped from Italy when he set off for his return to England.

But however much or little Milton read of Florentine Platonism, he inevitably met it in English writers. Under

---

[12] On the identity of reason and virtue, see note 11 above; cf. Spenser, *Faerie Queene* 2. 11. 1-2; and for the whole concept of rational freedom see Muirhead's analysis of the doctrines of the Cambridge Platonists, as given above.

Ficino's direction the Florentine Academy had turned its interest in Plato into a cult, which quickly spread. It reached Oxford, chiefly through Thomas Linacre; captured the interest of Colet, Erasmus, More, and Eliot; and with Erasmus' teaching at Cambridge became the philosophy that was to dominate Sidney, Spenser, and a whole generation of English poets.

When Sir John Cheke taught 'Cambridge and King Edward Greek,' he taught very largely the Greek of Plato and added the Latin Platonism of Ficino.[13] So too with Erasmus, Ascham, and More. All were under the spell of Plato, and it was Ficino who cast the Platonic spell upon them all. The matter is too generally agreed upon to need further comment.[14] What interests us is to see with what sympathy and approval Milton always speaks of these transmitters of Italian Platonism, especially Erasmus. Perhaps Bacon too may be linked with the group since, like Giordano Bruno, Ramus, and Galileo, he brought a kind of Platonism to oppose the contemporary Aristotelianism.[15] The interest Milton took in this latter group squarely contradicts Agar's view. And through the Elizabethan poets, his tie to Renaissance Platonism is even stronger. In Sidney, for example, we find a temperament, at once Platonic and Protestant, very like Milton's own.

But obviously the strongest tie is with Spenser, whom Milton acknowledged as his 'original' (18. 381). Scholars

---

[13] See Einstein, *The Italian Renaissance in England*, p. 345.

[14] For a succinct account of the introduction of Platonism into England see Kurt Schroeder, *Platonismus in der Englischen Renaissance vor und bei Thomas Eliot*, pp. 1-21.

[15] Against Bacon's vehement condemnation of Plato in *Temporis Partus Masculus* and some few other passages, may be set many favorable comments, among them the suggestion, in *Novum Organum* 1. 105, that Plato alone had glimpsed the true scientific method of induction. See also *Novum Organum* 2. 226; and *The Advancement of Learning* 3. 4 and 5. 4.

have begun to show how far the *Faerie Queene* was a model for *Paradise Lost*[16]; and like study will reveal a like use in *Comus* and *Paradise Regained*. Milton declared 'our admired Spenser' (3. 166-7) a 'better teacher than Scotus or Aquinas' (4. 311); and what Spenser taught, when not strictly Platonic, is the Platonism of Ficino, associated, as in Ficino himself, with matter drawn from Aristotle and Christianity.

As Augustine links Milton with the Christian mystics of his age who favored the Neoplatonism of Plotinus, so Spenser links him with contemporaries who drew their Platonism from Ficino. Agar rightly distinguishes Milton's purer understanding of Plato from much of the mystic and fanciful interpretation popular at the time. Yet in so far as Milton gave his admiration to Augustine and Spenser, we cannot think all the interpreters of Plato who preceded Milton alien to him. Indeed, he used Neoplatonic teachings as they did, and was no more sedulous than they to draw sharp lines between Platonism, Neoplatonism, and Christianity. The only distinction we can make between Milton and others in their reading of Plato comes simply to the inevitable difference between the clearer insight of a keener mind and the more confused impressions of the less gifted. The emphasis in Milton's use of Plato is certainly more on what is reasoned and analytic, less on the mythical and exuberant, than in other Platonists of the Renaissance; but they all use both aspects of the Dialogues. Only he, having greater power of analysis and reason, is more aware of the same powers in Plato.

---

[16] See especially Edwin Greenlaw, 'A Better Teacher than Aquinas,' *SP.* 14 (1917). 196-217; and 'Spenser's Influence on *Paradise Lost*,' *SP.* 17 (1920). 320-59.

CHAPTER III

'Himself a True Poem'

Milton's enthusiasm for the Platonic teaching left its mark on his theory of poetry. Even before he began his careful study of the Dialogues he had used Platonic myth and figure to adorn his verse, like most poets of the Renaissance. And again like them, he had recognized the poet in Plato. Thus he concluded his lines *De Idea Platonica* by addressing Plato:

But you, the unfading glory of the Academy—if you were the first to introduce such monsters [the Ideas] to the schools—surely you will recall the poets exiled from your State, for you are the greatest fabler of them all; or, founder though you be, you must yourself go forth. (MacKellar, p. 143.)

The lines show too that from the first Milton recognized in Plato's words on poetry a paradox. And though he came to think it only a seeming paradox, in coming to terms with the apparent inconsistency he gained, like the Platonists Sidney before and Shelley after him, a view of poetry that Plato often teaches. The paradox may indeed have been designed to that end. At any rate, Milton worked out a solution to the riddle.

To be sure, the view of poetry he thus came to hold was current in the Renaissance. But so too was Platonism. And we are here concerned with the direct impact of one great mind upon another, an impact that we know occurred, however it was prepared for in advance or later strengthened

45

by the influence of all the Platonists from Aristotle on down. In any event, it was far from common even in the Renaissance for a poet to say as Milton did:

> He who would not be frustrate of his hope to write well hereafter in laudable things ought himself to be a true Poem, that is, a composition and pattern of the best and honorablest things. (*Ap. Smect.* 3. 303.)

The definition of a true poem as a 'composition and pattern of the best and honorablest things' is extraordinary, and so too the assertion that a poet can communicate only what he himself is, and should therefore himself be such a composition of the good and honorable. Had Milton fed only on the Platonic critics of his age, he would not have thus identified poet, poem, and moral excellence.

What then is the paradox that had this influence on him? Simply, that Plato, himself a poet and an admirer of the poetic gift, condemned poetry. In other terms, it is the composite of the two things that every one knows Plato said about poetry: that poets are the inspired oracles of the gods and that poets ought to be banished from a perfect State. The two assertions are in the most obvious manner contradictory; if Plato held the one view, he could not in all piety have held the other. At any rate, he had somewhat more to say about poetry.

'Is not the test by which we always distinguish one art from another,' asks Socrates in the *Republic* 1. 346, 'its possession of different powers? And does not each of these arts give us a distinctive, and not a common, benefit?' To our knowledge, Plato never had his Socrates define the 'different powers' and 'distinctive benefit' of poetry. But everywhere he insisted that the true function and true form of an art are interchangeable, and that since the form is properly determined by the function, the function may not be abused without damage to the form. Further, when he banished poetry from his ideal State, he gave as chief reason its damaging effect on the audience, thus stating decisively— if in negative terms—that the ultimate function of poetry, as of every activity, must be to make men better. What Plato did, in effect, was to question the right of an art to exist in opposition to the end of all other human activity, the happiness that, according to him, is won only through the wisdom synonomous with virtue.

What then of the poet's divine inspiration? If his words are to be judged by the same measure as all the more prosaic utterances of lawyer and schoolmaster, that is, by the measure in which they inculcate the habits of thought that promote harmonious living, what sense can there be in calling his words divinely inspired? No sense at all in calling the words so, but much in so naming the gift; for in exiling poets lest they corrupt his citizenry, the Platonic Socrates paid them an unusual tribute inasmuch as he credited them with the power of swaying others to share their views. But, however inspired he thought the poetic capacity, he did not think that ended the matter. On the contrary, when he chose to dismiss the poets as irrelevant, in the *Apology* for example, he called them inspired madmen; but when he had them up for the test, in the *Republic* and the *Laws,* he asked how sanely they were using their inspiration.

The word that solves the riddle of Plato's statements on poetry is *teaching*. The poets could teach—that he never questioned; their persuasive power was god-given. But did they know that they were teachers, and to what they should persuade? And here he did question—with what effect Milton bears witness.

Milton, who saw how much a poet Plato himself was, at first refused to take the condemnation of poetry seriously. He much preferred the doctrine of poetic inspiration. And little wonder! Here is the vindication of the poet's vision

47

and rapture. He is told that his Utopian fancies are nearer to reality than other men's humdrum reasonings, and that the capacity to see and speak those fancies is divine. What ardent maker of verses will deny the compliment? To Milton, fresh from rereading *Phaedrus,* the language of divine inspiration was highly acceptable. Thus he writes to his close friend Diodati in the letter previously quoted:

> Though I know not God's intent toward me in other respects, yet of this I am sure, that he has imbued me especially with a mighty passion for Beauty. Ceres never sought her daughter Proserpine (as the legend tells) with greater ardor than I do this Idea of Beauty, like some image of loveliness; ever pursuing it, by day and by night, in every shape and form ('for many forms there are of things divine') and following close in its footprints as it leads. . . . What am I thinking about? you ask. So help me God, of immortality. What am I doing? Growing wings and learning to fly; but my Pegasus can only rise on tender pinions as yet, so let my new wisdom be humble. (Tillyard, p. 14.)

He is as inspired as the best of them, and as certain that the realm his Pegasus will climb to is the realm of Beauty Absolute.

Earlier too, in his Sixth *Elegy,* he had spoken of the poet as an oracle:

> But the poet who tells of wars, and of heaven under Jove to manhood grown, of pious heroes, and of demigods, the leaders of men—who sings now of the sacred decrees of the gods above, and now of that deep realm guarded by the barking dog—he indeed must live sparely, after the manner of the Samian master, and herbs must supply his harmless fare. Let only the crystal-clear water in a beechen bowl stand near him, and let him drink temperate draughts from the pure spring. More than this, his youth must be chaste and free from sin, his manners strict, and his hand without stain, even like you, O priest, when in sacred vestment and gleaming with the waters of cleansing you rise as

augur to face the angry gods. . . . Truly the bard is sacred to the gods; he is their priest, and both his heart and lips mysteriously breathe the indwelling Jove. (MacKellar, pp. 99-101.)

And similarly in *Ad Patrem:*

Scorn not the poet's song, a work divine, which more than aught else reveals our ethereal origin and heavenly race. Nothing so much as its origin does grace to the human mind, possessing yet some sacred traces of Promethean fire. (*Ibid.,* pp. 143-5.)

But though these passages recall the accounts of poetic inspiration in *Ion* (534) and *Phaedrus* (244-7), they tell less about how the poet is to achieve his sublime function than does the letter to Diodati. In the Sixth *Elegy* Milton sets mysterious hurdles for himself; in the letter he has at least to pursue the Idea in every shape and form. In *Ad Patrem* the 'poet's song' is by its very nature 'a work divine'; in the letter its divinity has to be won.

And even so, the letter to Diodati bespeaks the young Platonist, and it took an older, wiser student of the Dialogues to write *Paradise Lost, Paradise Regained,* and *Samson Agonistes.* Much that had been satisfactory to the youth at Horton became inadequate to the man in middle life watching his country in civil turmoil. Like any thoughtful man, he was aware of the contradiction between what humanity might be and what it is; and circumstances did not permit him to remain half aware. The strife in England forbade unconcerned pursuit of the seemingly remote path of artistic achievement. If the world was awry, men of vision must set it right. And who were the men of vision if not such as he? It was as visionary power that he had thought his poetic talent divine, and because it was to give him sight beyond men's actual lot, insight into what their lot might and should be, that he had sought the Idea of Beauty. His first duty, then, was to lend his eyes to the State. So Milton chose to do.

But the choice meant a departure from his once-chosen path, if only because a man cannot at the same time be doing two distinct kinds of work. Either poetry must become his pleasant avocation in leisure hours, or he must cease to be an active poet. If Milton had thought poetry a mere personal indulgence, he could have been content; or if he had thought it the most important activity of human life, he could have ignored the troubles of politics for the nobler calling. But Milton thought neither the true role of poetry.

Yet poetry could hardly be an occupation for men living in a settled and perfected state of society; for the times are always somewhat out of joint, and the tasks of civic life endless even when they are not tasks of military performance. The institutions which men in their occasional spurts of vision create, and in their long centuries of folly pervert, are always in some need of correction. When would a poet ever be freed by the stability of society to be a poet? Yet a poet Milton felt himself to be, and only at second best a statesman or political theorist. Somehow he must reconcile with the more obvious duty the career to which he had first pledged himself.

The *Reason of Church-Government* records how Milton made that reconciliation. What he there says is relevant to our search, because Plato's theory of poetry gave him the argument by which he could assign to poetry the rank of means, not end, and still justify himself as a poet. Let us consider the relevant passages step by step.

The work starts with a principle from Plato's *Laws*, which Milton intends to apply to the matter in hand:

In the publishing of human laws, which for the most part aim not beyond the good of civil society, to set them barely forth to the people without reason or preface, like a physical prescript, or only with threatenings, as it were a lordly command, in the judgment of Plato was thought to be done neither gen-

erously nor wisely. His advice was, seeing that persuasion certainly is a more winning and more manlike way to keep men
in obedience than fear, that to such laws as were of principal
moment there should be used as an induction some well-tempered
discourse, showing how good, how gainful, how happy it must
needs be to live according to honesty and justice; which being
uttered with those native colors and graces of speech, as true
eloquence, the daughter of virtue, can best bestow upon her
mother's praises, would so incite, and in a manner charm the
multitude into the love of that which is really good as to embrace
it ever after, not of custom and awe, which most men do, but
of choice and purpose, with true and constant delight. (3. 181.)

The principle, Milton hastens to add, is not Plato's alone;
he finds this 'point of so high wisdom and worth' in the
Mosaic law, as well as in the *Laws* of 'the wisest of the
heathen.' Plato thus has the sanction of consistency with
Holy Writ; or, as we might say, the important point is not
that it was Plato who said this, but that what he said is
true.

This doctrine, that persuasion is a better instrument than
force for the improvement of men, becomes the basis of
Milton's further argument in the *Reason of Church-Government* on the place of the Church and of Churchmen in
political life, and later the basis of his arguments on government, marriage, education, and censorship. The doctrine,
that is to say, becomes central to his thought; it is of the
highest importance in his theory of poetry.

The Second Book of the *Reason of Church-Government*
begins with the declaration that the man of knowledge
would indeed be happy if his knowledge did not carry with
it the burden of spreading the truth he knows, and that in
the face of men's frequent hostility to truth. Lest his reader
ask, 'What truth?' Milton prevents the question by distinguishing between understanding of fact ('that knowledge
that rests in the contemplation of natural causes and dimen-

sions, which must needs be a lower wisdom, as the object is low') and the knowledge which we might call insight ('of God, and of his true worship, and what is infallibly good and happy in the state of man's life, what in itself evil and miserable, though vulgarly not so esteemed'). The distinction is much the same as Plato made between the realms of Becoming and Being, or as we might make between the studies of physics and ethics. The point to note is that Milton and Plato attribute much greater importance to ethical than to physical knowledge.

Now since this burden of education is imposed on the philosophical mind, Milton—though he may seem 'too inquisitive or suspicious' of himself and his doings—feels that such ability as God has entrusted to him was intended to be used on just such occasions as this present dispute on Church-affairs. Otherwise his conscience might say through the rest of life:

> Thou hadst the diligence, the parts, the language of a man, if a vain subject were to be adorned or beautified; but when the cause of God and his Church was to be pleaded, for which purpose that tongue was given thee which thou hast, God listened, . . . but thou wert dumb as a beast; from henceforward be that which thine own brutish silence hath made thee. (3. 232-3.)

Briefly, Milton feels that not to enter this controversy on the gravest of human concerns would condemn him to think poetry, what many do think it, the 'vain adorning and beautifying of vain things.' If he chooses, then, to write with his 'left hand,' knowing himself in such controversy to be inferior to himself in his native medium of poetry, it is because a poet's right concerns are not with vanity, but with things of the highest seriousness. And on this point he may permit himself to expatiate.

Thus we come to Milton's *apologia* for poetry, which begins, appropriately enough, with an account of his own poetic training, significant in its emphasis on the discipline which a poet must undergo, on the 'labor and intent study' which he must take to be his 'portion in this life' even if given 'the strong propensity of nature.' The career of the poet, we are to understand, cannot be lightly undertaken; nor was it by Milton. His regard is to God's glory 'by the honor and instruction' of his country; his purpose, 'not to make verbal curiosities the end (that were a toilsome vanity), but to be an interpreter and relater of the best and sagest things among mine own citizens.' (Observe how that *best and sagest* prefigures the definition of poetry in the *Apology for Smectymnuus* as 'a pattern of the best and honorablest things.')

After enumerating the poetic types and subjects through which such an aim might be fulfilled, Milton goes on to argue that such is the aim, not simply of the poet Milton, but of poetry, that this function of interpreting and relating 'the best and sagest things' is not arbitrarily assigned by him, but proper to the talents which we call poetic.

Before we quote in its entirety the next passage, in which Milton pretty well condenses his whole theory of poetry, let us remind ourselves of the argument with which the *Reason of Church-Government* opened, that persuasion is a better educational instrument than force. Now if man is to be persuaded to goodness, clearly the poet, who shares with the orator the talent for persuasive utterance, may take his place beside lawgiver, educator, and spiritual adviser, beside all who seek to improve human life—if the poet understands his own powers and the use to be made of them. Thus Milton:

These abilities, wheresoever they be found, are the inspired gift of God, rarely bestowed, but yet to some (though most abuse) in every nation; and are of power, beside the office of a pulpit, to inbreed and cherish in a great people the seeds of virtue and public civility, to allay the perturbations of the mind, and set the affections in right tune; to celebrate in glorious and lofty hymns the throne and equipage of God's almightiness, and what He works, and what He suffers to be wrought with high providence in his Church; to sing the victorious agonies of martyrs and saints, the deeds and triumphs of just and pious nations doing valiantly through faith against the enemies of Christ; to deplore the general relapses of kingdoms and states from justice and from God's true worship. Lastly, whatsoever in religion is holy and sublime, in virtue amiable or grave, whatsoever hath passion or admiration in all the changes of that which is called fortune from without, or the wily subtleties and refluxes of man's thoughts from within; all these things with a solid and treatable smoothness to paint out and describe— teaching over the whole book of sanctity and virtue through all the instances of example, with such delight to those especially of soft and delicious temper, who will not so much as look upon truth herself unless they see her elegantly dressed; that whereas the paths of honesty and good life appear now rugged and difficult, though they be indeed easy and pleasant, they would then appear to all men both easy and pleasant, though they were rugged and difficult indeed. (3. 238-9.)

For Milton too, it seems, the reconciling word is teaching. And for good reasons, not least among them that the source of this passage is in Plato's *Laws*. There, in a discussion of poetry, the Athenian Stranger had come upon the problem that led Socrates in the *Republic* to outlaw poets, and had resolved it by a more limited—and yet more rigorous because more seriously intended—censorship. The problem is this, Will they, won't they, poets do teach. The solution is: let them be told what they must teach. And hence the Athenian Stranger lists the kinds of poem to be composed.

It will be most fitting to address the gods in hymns and strains of praise and prayer commingled; and, after the gods, there should be offered prayers and praises in like manner to the demigods and heroes, as severally befits them. . . . Thereafter we may at once proceed without demur to the following regulation.

All citizens who have brought to an end a life of honorable toil, of bodily or spiritual achievement, and been obedient to the laws, shall be considered fitting objects of our praises. . . . But those who are still living it is not safe to honor with hymns and panegyrics; it is not safe till a man has finished his course, and reached a noble end. . . .

Delight is common to all styles of composition. What counts is whether a man has been reared, from childhood up to the age of firm good sense, in music that is sane and orderly; if so, he is repelled whenever he hears the opposite kind, and calls it vulgar; whereas if he has been reared on music of the common sugary sort, he declares that its opposite is frigid and unpleasing. Accordingly, as I was saying, in respect of the pleasure or dissatisfaction either type affords, neither takes precedence of the other; the real superiority lies herein, that one type always makes those who are reared in it better, while the other makes them worse. (*Laws* 7. 801-2. Cooper, pp. 400-2.)

The passages from Plato and Milton are alike, especially in their lists of approved subjects. Where Plato has (1) hymns and praises of the gods, Milton makes only the change required by monotheism; for (2) the pagan demi-gods and heroes to whom prayers and praises are to be addressed, Milton substitutes Christian saints and martyrs; (3) the private citizens, the individuals of Plato's City-state, who are to be the subjects of eulogy give way to the 'just and pious nations' of Milton's more cosmopolitan scheme; and (4) where Plato would have no man celebrated before his death, lest he lapse from virtue, Milton thinks the very lapses 'from justice and God's true worship' become fit subjects if properly deplored.

Such a parallel comes neither by accident nor by servile imitation. Milton has taken to mind what the Athenian said, has weighed its worth, added what he found wanting, and canceled what he thought amiss. He dismisses with the words 'though most abuse' the whole condemnation of un-

55

licensed poetic practice which occurs just before the passage here quoted from the *Laws* and ends with the words, 'Taken as a whole, the poets are not so very capable of discerning what is good and what is not.' He changes Plato's legislation. The Athenian would decree that:

No poet shall write any poem that conflicts with what, in accordance with the public standard, is right and lawful, beautiful and good; nor show his compositions to any private individual until they have been submitted to the appointed judges in these matters, and to the guardians of the law, and been officially approved. (*Laws* 7. 801. Cooper, p. 400.)

For Milton, not the legislator's edict, but the nature of poetry suggests whatsoever is 'holy and sublime' as fit for poets 'to paint out and describe.' And finally, where Plato still doubtful of the poet's ability to keep this high aim, declares that either the good or the bad may become delightful through habit, Milton puts it positively as the poet's native function 'to inbreed and cherish . . . the seeds of virtue and public civility.' Plato says this can be the effect of a poetry properly guided by law; Milton asserts that it is the effect proper to poetry.

But obviously he can assert no such thing in the face of what actual poets often do, which Plato had considered before deciding that they need legislative restraint. Milton may dispense with the suggested restraint, but cannot blink the fact. He puts his stress therefore on the nature of poetry, 'though most abuse'; and of the abuses speaks no more gently than Plato.

The passage in the *Reason of Church-Government* goes on:

And what a benefit this would be to our youth and gentry may be soon guessed by what we know of the corruption and bane which they suck in daily from the writings and interludes of libidinous and ignorant poetasters, who having scarce ever heard of that which is the main consistence of a true poem, the choice of such persons as they ought to introduce, and what is moral and decent to each one, do for the most part lap up vicious principles in sweet pills to be swallowed down, and make the taste of virtuous documents harsh and sour.

This being true, perhaps the Athenian law-giver was right after all, and the State should concern itself with poetry. At least Milton feels it necessary to add:

But because the spirit of man cannot demean itself lively in this body without some recreating intermission of labor and serious things, it were happy for the commonwealth if our magistrates, as in those famous governments of old, would take into their care, not only the deciding of our contentious law-cases and brawls, but the managing of our public sports and festival pastimes; that they might be, not such as were authorized a while since, the provocations of drunkenness and lust, but such as may inure and harden our bodies by martial exercises to all warlike skill and performance; and may civilize, adorn, and make discreet our minds by the learned and affable meeting of frequent academies and the procurement of wise and artful recitations, sweetened with eloquent and graceful enticements to the love and practice of justice, temperance, and fortitude, instructing and bettering the nation at all opportunities, that the call of wisdom and virtue may be heard everywhere, as Solomon saith. . . . Whether this may not be, not only in pulpits, but after another persuasive method, at set and solemn paneguries, in theatres, porches, or what other place or way may win most upon the people to receive at once both recreation and instruction, let them in authority consult.

There can be no question that Milton had been reading the *Laws*. Though 'Solomon saith' in *Proverbs* (i. 20-1), 'Wisdom crieth without; she uttereth her voice in the streets; she crieth in the chief place of concourse, in the openings of the gates'; it was Plato's Athenian Stranger who gave edicts on how she might best use her voice, naming the administrators, the occasions, and the public as-

57

semblies in which she was to be heard, almost exactly as Milton names them.

The details of those edicts need not be retold here; for far more significant than any borrowing of details is Milton's acceptance, with modification, of the principles involved. With modification, be it noted, because while the Athenian would have the wrong kind of poetry forbidden by statute, Milton urges only that the right kind be encouraged by 'them in authority.' Why he rejected the negative decree we shall better understand when we come to his treatment of Plato's censorship in *Areopagitica*.

Here, in the *Reason of Church-Government*, Milton has applied the declaration of Plato, that persuasion is superior to force, more thoroughly than Plato himself ever attempted to do. Not by force of censorship, but by persuasion to civic duty, the State shall set the poet to a right use of his inspired abilities. Milton himself intends to encourage poets by the persuasive force of his example. Now that he is satisfied with the poet's high mission, he has absolved himself from the suspicion of vanity, of remoteness from the important issues of life, or of concern with such poetry as may be 'raised from the heat of youth or the vapors of wine, like that which flows at waste from the pen of some vulgar amorist, or the trencher fury of a rhyming parasite.' He now may 'covenant with any knowing reader' to produce at some future time just such poetry as he has described as poetry proper—granted always that 'by devout prayer' he may continue to receive the divine inspiration, and that by 'industrious and select reading, steady observation, insight into all seemly and generous arts and affairs' he perseveres in training that inspiration into the ways of art. The time is not yet, because the effects of poetry are ultimate and the immediate effects of rhetoric are at present needed, but the path of his return to poetry has been cleared of the last conscientious doubt.

Plato having offered the alternatives of poetry in the service of morality or no poetry at all, Milton, though he denied the alternative, accepted the duty, and having accepted, fulfilled it to the letter in *Paradise Lost, Paradise Regained,* and *Samson Agonistes.* Poetry has now a function other than, yet not unconnected with, the revelation of the Beautiful, a work to be done in the realms of true doctrine and social good as well. Milton therefore may still think of himself as a poet; and while he continues to write pamphlets because of immediate necessity, he may bide his time with no sense that the pull in him towards poetry is a pull away from his responsibilities as man and citizen. He has found his own bent justified by the same philosopher who had described the pursuit of Ideal Beauty.

On the didactic function of poetry, Milton and Plato are thus agreed. But what of the didactic effect of bad poetry? If Plato was right to count poetry among the instruments of teaching, how can Milton deny the ill done by those poets who are 'not so very capable of discerning what is good and what is not'? As we have seen, he makes no attempt to deny the evil, but abjures the means by which Plato's Utopian polities would prevent it. We have, in other words, still to consider *Areopagitica,* which seems a flat repudiation of all that Plato had to say on poetry, inasmuch as it repudiates the censorship prescribed in the *Laws* no less than the dismissal of poets in the *Republic.* Indeed, Milton rightly fixes his attention on the *Laws* as the serious utterance which advocates of censorship might cite:

Plato, a man of high authority indeed, but least of all for his Commonwealth, in the book of his *Laws,* which no city ever yet received, fed his fancy with making many edicts to his airy burgomasters, which they who otherwise admire him, wish had been rather buried and excused in the genial cups of an Academic night sitting. By which laws he seems to tolerate no kind of learning but by unalterable decree, consisting most of practical traditions, to the attainment whereof a library of smaller bulk than his own Dialogues would be abundant; and there also enacts that no poet should so much as read to any private man what he had written, until the judges and law-keepers had seen it and allowed it. (4. 316.)

What follows then for Milton, who 'otherwise admired' Plato? Not simple defiance, but an attempt to extricate some ground of agreement:

But that Plato meant this law peculiarly to that commonwealth which he had imagined, and to no other, is evident. Why was he not else a law-giver to himself, but a transgressor, and to be expelled by his own magistrates, both for the wanton epigrams and dialogues which he made, and his perpetual reading of Sophron, Mimus, and Aristophanes, books of grossest infamy; and also for commending the latter of them, though he were the malicious libeler of his chief friends, to be read by the tyrant Dionysius, who had little need of such trash to spend his time on? But that he knew this licensing of poems had reference and dependence to many other provisos there set down in his fancied republic, which in this world could have no place; and so neither he himself, nor any magistrate or city, ever imitated that course, which, taken apart from those other collateral injunctions, must needs be vain and fruitless.

Obviously the insistence that Plato is really of Milton's party may be mere polemic. It is well in pushing an argument to reinterpret the authorities your opponent may cite, and to make them, if you can, sanction your own view. But why drag Plato in at all unless you acknowledge his authority? Or why not, if Plato's name can be hurled against you, hurl back Aristotle's? Instead, Milton elaborates the discussion in *Areopagitica*—because, we surmise, he wanted to agree with Plato if he could. He goes on to show that the laws of censorship in the Dialogues are not rightly understood apart from their context:

If we think to regulate printing, thereby to rectify manners, we must regulate all recreations and pastimes, all that is delightful to man. No music must be heard, no song be set or sung, but what is grave and Doric. There must be licensing dancers, that no gesture, motion, or deportment be taught our youth, but what by their allowance shall be thought honest; for such Plato was provided of.

But 'provided of,' Milton reminds us, as a poet for a mythical realm, not as a legislator for an existing community. And here he uses the most severe words of all:

To sequester out of the world into Atlantic and Utopian polities, which can never be drawn into use, will not mend our condition, but to ordain wisely as in this world of evil, in the midst whereof God hath placed us unavoidably. (4. 318.)

Now if Milton had thought Plato a mere 'Utopian' who 'fed his fancy with making many edicts to his airy burgomasters' (an 'escapist' to use our term), we should have to revise our whole preceding argument, and say that after he had written *The Reason of Church-Government* Milton came to see how wrong the whole Platonic theory of poetry was. Milton was not one to approve the sentimental turn of mind which takes refuge in impossible phantasy. But then, no more was Plato; and Milton knew it. Indeed, he knew perfectly well that Plato knew what a Utopia is for, and he states the knowledge with every mark of assent, though not in *Areopagitica*. In the *Apology for Smectymnuus* he had praised

that grave and noble invention which the greatest and sublimest wits in sundry ages, Plato in *Critias*, and our own two famous countrymen, the one in his *Utopia*, the other in his *New Atlantis*, chose, I may not say as a field, but as a mighty continent wherein to display the largeness of their spirits by teaching this our world better and exacter things than were yet known or used. (3. 294.)

Utopias, then, have their practical bearing. So too may a Utopian censorship; but *Areopagitica* would hardly have been the work in which to stress the point. Yet even here Milton asserts—and surely admirers of Plato will agree—that an intelligent reader gains from the ideal States of Plato not an impossible set of legal prohibitions, but a way of regarding human life and of testing the worth of human aims. Milton ends the argument by pointing to what in the *Laws* (and doubtless the *Republic* too) best merits attention:

> Nor is it Plato's licensing of books will do this [that is, mend our condition], which necessarily pulls along with it so many other kinds of licensing as will make us all both ridiculous and weary, and yet frustrate; but those unwritten, or at least unconstraining, laws of virtuous education, religious and civil nurture, which Plato there mentions as the bonds and ligaments of the commonwealth, the pillars and the sustainers of every written statute, these they be which will bear chief sway in such matters as these, when all licensing will be easily eluded. (4. 318.)

But what precisely are these 'unwritten, or at least unconstraining, laws of virtuous education' and the rest, to which Milton would allow 'chief sway in such matters as these'? They seem to this student of the *Laws* very nearly the same as those of censorship, or rather simply their converse. When the Athenian Stranger discusses the kinds of music the State will encourage, he implicitly, and explicitly too, rejects every other. Milton seems to have led us to a paradox of his own every bit as puzzling as Plato's. For the great difference would seem to be that Milton would have censorship by encouragement, and specifically in the realms of 'education, religious and civil nurture'; Plato, by encouragement and discouragement both, and throughout all realms of life. And how slight a difference that comes to a few minutes of thought would have led Milton to see—if he had believed that Plato meant his censorship to be a legal prescription at all. He did not; he thought the explicit legalities a challenge rather than a prescription, and right as a challenge where they would be wrong as a prescription. He took this transfer of censorship from external law to internal education to be in the spirit of Plato's intention, and on the need of such censorship agreed with Plato. The poet is to keep himself at his proper work, and the reader to guard himself against the mistakes of wrong poetry.

How the principle would work we may see in *Paradise Regained,* when just after Satan's magnificent encomium of classical literature, to the distress of a good many readers, Jesus replies censoriously:

> Think not but that I know these things; or think
> I know them not, not therefore am I short
> Of knowing what I ought: he who receives
> Light from above, from the fountain of light,
> No other doctrine needs, though granted true;
> But these are false, or little else but dreams,
> Conjectures, fancies, built on nothing firm. . . .
> Who therefore seeks in these
> True wisdom, finds her not, or by delusion
> Far worse, her false resemblance only meets,
> An empty cloud. However, many books
> Wise men have said are wearisome; who reads
> Incessantly, and to his reading brings not
> A spirit and judgment equal or superior,
> (And what he brings, what needs he elsewhere seek)
> Uncertain and unsettl'd still remains,
> Deep verst in books and shallow in himself.
>
> (4. 286-92, 318-27.)

Intolerable as the doctrine sounds, and especially intolerable from Milton, who could not have written even these lines if he had not himself read the pagan classics, Jesus' speech has a meaning, and Milton agreed with it. If you have the perfect in a Platonic Republic or by a direct and complete participation in the divine mind, of what use can the imperfect be to you? Moreover, how can you be in

63

need of it? But, of course, if you do not have the perfect revelation of truth, or perfect poems, or a perfectly working life for all the members of your State, the answer must be different. Milton can use and does need the classics, as Plato needed and could use Sophron, 'Mimus,' and Aristophanes. And yet we do well to keep in mind what the perfect truth and the perfect poem would be, if only as a standard by which to judge what in the imperfect is to be assimilated and what in it the assimilating mind should reject. The meaning of Plato's censorship, as Milton took it, like the meaning of Jesus' speech on classical learning is: Be wary if you read, even warier if you write.

For both Milton and Plato, then, poetry is doctrine, whether true or false, with a fearful power of influence. Plato seems to stress the fearful side, Milton the power; and yet both see the same duty and the same danger. For both the poet is a teacher, not because they thought poorly of poetry, but because they thought astonishingly well of teaching. When Milton says 'what religious, what glorious and magnificent, use might be made of poetry both in divine and human things' (Ainsworth, p. 60), he ascribes a didactic function to art as surely as Plato did.

But when Milton says that poets can teach, and therefore should teach wisely, he no more means than Plato did that the poet is to be for ever conning over the maxims of copy-book morality. 'Teaching over the *whole* book of sanctity and virtue' is his phrase. If we think of a small book and an unimaginative preceptor, Milton is hardly at fault. He meant all virtue by 'virtue,' not temperance alone, and by 'sanctity' the wholeness and health which are the prerequisites to, if not indeed the essence of, a full and joyous life. He meant by poetry's teaching what Wordsworth meant by 'truth carried alive into the heart by passion'; by 'sanctity and virtue,' Sidney's 'ending end of all earthly

64

learning'; and by the 'whole book' of it, Shelley's 'very image of life expressed in its eternal truth.'

De Quincey would have it that the cookery-book teaches while *Paradise Lost* moves. Yet the cookery-book moves the gourmand; and *Paradise Lost* taught De Quincey, by moving him to think Milton's thought and affirm Milton's values—as far as De Quincey could. Neither Plato nor Milton ever said that the poet must remember to add a moral to the story. Indeed, Milton quoted Plato as objecting to the acceptance of moral commonplaces from 'custom and awe, which most men do,' and insisting that the good to be really good must be deliberately chosen 'with true and constant delight.' They thought the whole story a continuous revelation of morality, good or bad; that what the heart affirms the mind too will come to believe—and act upon; that, as Milton put it, doctrine and discipline are one. And hence the truth or falsehood cherished by the poet inevitably leaves its impress on his poetry, and his poetry, if it is successful, on his audience; for if the poet makes us sympathize, he inevitably makes us sympathize with better or with worse modes of thought, feeling, and behavior. And if he makes us sympathize wrongly, he works against what all wise men work for, and abuses a power greater than others possess.

Thus the Athenian of the *Laws* argued when he fancied himself addressing the poets:

'Most estimable Strangers,' we shall say, 'we ourselves are the authors of a tragedy, at once the finest and the best we can compose. At any rate our polity has all been framed in *imitation of the best and fairest life*; which, as for us, we hold to be in very fact the truest tragedy. Thus if you are poets, then we too are poets, makers of the self-same things, rivals in your art.' (*Laws* 7. 817. Cooper, p. 417. The italics are mine.)

Milton, far from quarreling with this view of poetry, goes

65

along with Plato in the last, hardest step of all to the conviction that we can teach others only what we ourselves are. The poet's task, therefore, is not for every one who can turn rhymes. Plato's lawgiver had said:

Herein not every one shall be an author; no, first the poet must not be under fifty years of age; nor, again, shall they compose who, though they have within themselves the gift of poetry and music, have never yet performed one noble and illustrious deed. But they who in themselves are good, and are honored in the State as artists in the doing of fair deeds, their poems may be sung even if the natural music should be lacking. (*Laws* 7. 829. Cooper, p. 418.)

Milton deliberately approves the passage, and rightly connects it with the definition of true tragedy as the 'imitation of the best and fairest life.'

To be sure, there is no reference to Plato in the Tractate *Of Education* when Milton speaks of

that sublime art which in Aristotle's *Poetics,* in Horace, and the Italian commentaries of Castelvetro, Tasso, Mazzoni, and others, teaches what the laws are of a true epic poem, what of a dramatic, what of a lyric, what decorum is—which is the grand masterpiece to observe. (Ainsworth, p. 60.)

But if nothing is said of learning the ultimate function of poetry from Plato, the earlier study of ethics may have taken care of that, and the study of rhetoric out of 'the rule of Plato' may reinforce the teaching. And in any event the course in poetic theory is to enable the student to perceive what religious, what glorious and magnificent, use might be made of poetry both in divine and human things.

That use is not pleasure alone. In *Paradise Lost,* Milton puts it that

Eloquence the Soul, Song charms the Sense. (2. 556.)

The line expresses the central concept of *Phaedrus,* that rhetoric is the art of enchanting the soul. And poetry is own sister to rhetoric in enchantment. Aristotle, Horace, and the rest will explain how the art succeeds or fails in casting the spell, but Plato tells what spell is to be cast. Moreover, after all the principles have been given—on epic, dramatic, and lyric poetry, and on decorum—the place to start from has still to be told. Like Plato, Milton thought it best to start from the truth to be expressed, by feeding on

> Thoughts that voluntary move
> Harmonious numbers. (*Paradise Lost* 3. 37-8.)

If the aim is to charm the hearer into the ways of good life, then the poet must begin by nourishing that life in himself. That is the gist of Plato's poetics from *Phaedrus* through the *Laws*. And Milton summarizes the whole Platonic argument when he declares:

And long it was not after, when I was confirmed in this opinion, that he who would not be frustrate of his hope to write well hereafter in laudable things, ought himself to be a true Poem, that is, a composition and pattern of the best and honorablest things, not presuming to sing high praises of heroic men or famous cities unless he have in himself the experience and practice of all that which is praiseworthy.

To be a true poet, a man must live the good life.

CHAPTER IV

The Good Life: Pleasure, Wealth, Fame

W HEN Satan turns Jesus in *Paradise Regained* to behold 'Athens, the eye of Greece,' he uses as bait

Sage Philosophy. . .
From Heaven descended to the low-rooft house
Of Socrates.

Milton has allowed the temptation to begin with the best
of pagan thought, the philosophy of 'the wisest of the
heathen.' But, heathen still, the Socrates of the Dialogues
could guide Milton only within the limits set by Christianity. To be sure, the limits were flexible. With Christian
thought Platonized at least since Augustine, the dividing
line is hard to fix even in theology. In ethics it becomes
imperceptible. And it was in ethics especially that Milton
followed Plato's leading, as the summary at the end of this
chapter indicates.

Investigators have already shown how deeply Plato
affected Milton's views on cosmology and music,[1] and we
may guess that studies of his politics and rhetoric would
yield similar results. But the chief effect was in the realm
of ethical thought. Perhaps, as Agar says, Milton and
Plato had 'an affinity of spirit,' though it is hard to de-

[1] See Sigmund Gottfried Spaeth, *Milton's Knowledge of Music;*
William Fairfield Warren, *The Universe as Pictured in Milton's Para-
dise Lost;* and Edward Chauncey Baldwin, 'Milton and Plato's
Timaeus,' PMLA. 35 (1920). 210-7.

cide where temperamental affinity ends and assimilation through study begins. Milton himself thought that study can create dispositions. And since we cannot hope to show how far his Platonic habits of thought were native, how far acquired, we had best be content to say merely how far they were Platonic.

Apparently Milton's own feeling was that the Dialogues gave him warrant for many of his views, and, in at least one particular, for personal habit. The reader will note in the appended table how often he comments on the Socratic jest. Sometimes, indeed, we could wish he had learned from Plato the gentleness that invariably tempers Socratic irony in the Dialogues; for the Miltonic jest cuts beyond the offense; and because his delight in satire often takes him too far for laughter, he is less successful than Plato in making error ludicrous.

But in assimilating the ethics of Plato he was more fortunate. We can watch his mind feeding on the Dialogues in the prose of his middle years, and in his later poetry see the result. The Platonism is no longer tagged in *Paradise Lost, Paradise Regained,* and *Samson Agonistes;* it is Milton's own. And now the influence has its real effect, being no longer in process of assimilation, but absorbed in the life-blood. But even those who deny that the mind can be nourished from without may find interest in marking how far these two sharp-sighted men see alike.

Milton, like Plato, was from early years concerned with the basic human question, what constitutes the good life? Like Plato again, he steadily examined the various aims that engage man's interest. His final choice among them is not Plato's, but in testing them he reveals a system of values remarkably akin to that of the Dialogues. It happens that both Plato and Milton took occasion at least once to sift a number of the goals men aim at, and measure their real contribution to happiness. Plato in the Eighth and Ninth

Books of the *Republic,* and Milton in *Paradise Regained,* test a series of human aims, reject with explanation all but one, and give us the principles by which the one exception is made the essential basis of human well-being. Throughout the writings of both, these goods are often dealt with and similarly judged, but here they are arranged in a scale, by Plato in descending order from best to worst, by Milton from lower to higher in the series of Jesus' temptations. It happens also that the two deal with very nearly the same list. As Plato traced the fall of the soul and the State from the aristocratic search for wisdom, through the timocratic love of fame and the democratic pursuit of wealth and then pleasure, to the final abyss of tyrannical hedonism, so Jesus conquers by renouncing pleasure, wealth, and power with its attendant fame, until at last he confronts the temptation of knowledge. The chance correspondence is important, but not essential. What matters most, what shows the heart of Plato's influence on Milton, is that they make very nearly the same judgment not only of the best, but of the worse and better.

PLEASURE

In Plato's scheme the life of pleasure corresponds to the rule of the lowest faculty of the soul. Appetite, the 'many-headed monster,' has three main desires: food, drink, and sexual gratification. None of these is bad in itself, although as they withdraw the soul from its chief concern they become obstacles to the highest life, that of philosophy. Still the evil is not in appetite, but in its resistance to control; and Plato takes care to distinguish between necessary and unnecessary desires, and between their attendant pleasures, honorable and dishonorable. In so far as every element in the soul seeks its proper object, each seeks pleasure; but while the higher objects afford the most intense delights,

71

Plato generally restricts the term ἡδονή to what pleases the sieve-like appetites. A life devoted to such gratification is the death of the spirit; for the anarchy of indulgence, although it seems at first to ask equal pleasure for all parts of the soul, eventually leads to the tyrannical destruction of the higher parts. When at length reason and will seek to balk undisciplined appetite, the 'many-headed monster,' which has been strengthened by feeding, kills off every better impulse, and thereafter lives for itself alone.

Whenever Plato allows pleasure to be a good at all, he means not the gratification of the senses however obtained, but what delights the best man, whose pleasure is a good and a test of the good in every other thing. In this sense pleasure and happiness may be identified, and Plato can deny that the tyranny of desire produces any enjoyment whatever. But in its more usual meaning, as the object of sensual appetite, pleasure is, of all possible ends, farthest removed from the highest good. Whatever meaning is given to the term, the kind of life generally called pleasant, that of unrestrained luxury, is the basest life a man may lead. Only when desire yields to reason, when pleasures are chosen by the standard of philosophy, can the senses properly be fed. Such a life we may call one of true enjoyment, but the measure of its joy is not in appetite.[2]

Milton, too, counts the pleasures of appetite the least of goods, and most likely to become a destructive force. His constant censure of Epicurean and Cyrenaic thought, his disdain of idolatrous ritual, and his high praise of temperance, all mark his distrust of the senses. 'Epicurus or that libertine school of Cyrene' for him, as the hedonism of a Callicles or Thrasymachus for Plato, represents the lowest kind of ethical doctrine. Similarly the feeding of the

---

[2] See *Republic* 9. 581-7; *Laws* 5. 732-4; also *Protagoras, Gorgias,* and *Philebus.*

senses in religious service, the pleasures afforded to sight, hearing, and smell, are in his view, no fit accompaniment to worship, but divert the worshiper from serious contemplation of God to idolatry. Hedonism is thus the perversion of ethics, and idolatry of religion, for the same reason: they pamper what they should restrain. In *Of Reformation* Milton argues against the Roman Catholic service:

> Faith [needs] not the weak and fallible office of the senses to be either the ushers or interpreters of heavenly mysteries, save where our Lord himself in his sacraments ordained. (3. 1-2.)

He uses the imagery of *Phaedrus* to describe the effect that sensuous pleasures have had upon religious rites:

> The Soul by this means of over-bodying herself, given up justly to fleshly delights, bated her wing apace downward; and finding the ease she had from her visible and sensuous colleague the body in performance of religious duties, her pinions now broken and flagging, shifted off from herself the labor of high soaring any more, forgot her heavenly flight, and left the dull and droiling carcass to plod on in the old road and drudging trade of outward conformity. (3. 2-3.)

We need not follow the polemic against religious formalism. Milton's position there is but the counterpart of his ethical doctrine on sensual pleasures, and we readily see that for him, as for Plato, loss of the wings of the soul is the invariable consequence of indulging the 'low inclinations of the senses.'

Comus is Milton's first hedonist. Corresponding to the Lady's virtue of chastity or the rule of reason, the vice of Comus is 'luxury' or the rule of pleasure. The image of men turned into beasts comes from Homer and Spenser, but Milton is Platonic in linking the transformation with sensual enjoyments. The court of Comus is the court of the 'many-headed monster' in both the Homeric and Platonic senses. Travelers wander into his realm and drink of his 'orient liquor,'

> which as they taste
> (For most do taste through fond intemperate thirst)
> Soon as the Potion works, their human count'nance,
> Th' express resemblance of the gods, is chang'd
> Into some brutish form. . . .
> And they, so perfect is their misery,
> Not once perceive their foul disfigurement,
> But boast themselves more comely than before,
> And all their friends, and native home forget
> To roul with pleasure in a sensual sty. (66-77.)

Of the uncontrolled delight in meats and drinks, the Lady says:

> If every just man that now pines with want
> Had but a moderate and beseeming share
> Of that which lewdly-pamper'd Luxury
> Now heaps upon some few with vast excess,
> Nature's full blessings would be well dispens't
> In unsuperfluous even proportion. (767-72.)

Thus the social as well as the individual effects of hedonism are the antithesis of good. So Plato held, and made the tyranny of appetite the lowest order not only for the soul but for the State.

But obviously the basest of pleasures is not that about which Comus and the Lady argue. Milton makes clear that the final degradation of the soul comes not from over-indulgence in food and drink, but

> when lust
> By unchaste looks, loose gestures, and foul talk,
> But most by lewd and lavish act of sin,
> Lets in defilement.

Then at length,

> The soul grows clotted by contagion,
> Imbodies, and imbrutes, till she quite lose
> The divine property of her first being. (462-8.)

THE GOOD LIFE: PLEASURE, WEALTH, FAME

In *Comus* Milton rejects pleasure as a good without any hesitation. But *Comus,* as we have said before, stems more from Spenser than from Plato.

In *Paradise Lost* there is a more Platonic distinction between necessary and unnecessary desires, pleasures right and wrong. Belial, a magnified Comus, comes last among the fallen angels,

> than whom a Spirit more lewd
> Fell not from Heaven, or more gross to love
> Vice for itself. (1. 490-2.)

His was the worship when

> Ely's Sons . . . fill'd
> With lust and violence the house of God.
> In Courts and Palaces he also Reigns
> And in luxurious Cities, where the noise
> Of riot ascends above their loftiest Tow'rs,
> And injury and outrage: And when Night
> Darkens the Streets, then wander forth the Sons
> Of Belial, flown with insolence and wine. (1. 495-502.)

Belial is thus the arch-hedonist, and Milton elsewhere describes 'the brood of Belial, the draff of men, to whom no liberty is pleasing but unbridled and vagabond lust' (3. 370).

But although pleasure taken as an end produces the monstrous Belial, pleasure subject to reason is not evil. Hence the large part accorded to sensual enjoyment in the Garden of Eden. Even the angelic hierarchy are not without senses and their delights, for hear Raphael's exposition of the manner of their enjoyment:

> What he [God] gives
> (Whose praise be ever sung) to man in part
> Spiritual, may of purest spirits be found
> No ingrateful food: and food alike those pure
> Intelligential substances require

75

As doth your Rational; and both contain
Within them every lower faculty
Of sense, whereby they hear, see, smell, touch, taste,
Tasting concoct, digest, assimilate,
And corporeal to incorporeal turn.
For know, whatever was created, needs
To be sustain'd and fed; of Elements
The grosser feeds the purer. (5. 404-16.)

The pleasures of sense, like the senses themselves, are of God's making, and are appointed to be the due satisfaction of natural desire. Only the perversion of values whereby the purer feeds the grosser results in the Comus-like perversion of incorporeal to corporeal. Milton's treatment of the love of Adam and Eve repeats this doctrine; the use of body is for spirit, of bodily delight for spiritual growth. Conversely, to separate bodily pleasure from, or magnify it above, spirit is to turn what God created good into evil. If we understand Milton's hierarchy of goods and his insistence that they be rigorously kept in order, we shall have no difficulty in reconciling the varied treatment of sensual pleasure in *Paradise Lost*. Nor shall we make the mistake, common among recent interpreters, of supposing that Milton exalts the goods of the body into an equality with goods of the soul.

The theme of Milton is constantly the theme of Plato:

Nothing is so native to men as pleasure, pain, and desire; they are, so to say, the very wires or strings from which any mortal nature is inevitably and absolutely dependent. We have therefore to commend the noble life, not only as superior in comeliness of repute, but further as superior, if a man will but taste it and not decline it in the days of his youth, in that on which we are all set, life-long predominance of pleasures over pains. (*Laws* 5. 732e-733a.)

Since the central issue of *Paradise Regained* is the winning of happiness, we may look there for Milton's more explicit judgment of the goods men have made their end. To be sure, all Satan offers must be temptation, and the dramatic fiction therefore allows Milton to discuss only false goods. Within the frame of the debate, he can show the true *summum bonum* only by implication and by denial of the lesser goods. Pleasure is the first of them to be ruled out. Belial's suggestion even Satan at once dismisses:

> Belial the dissolutest Spirit that fell,
> The sensuallest, and after Asmodai
> The fleshliest Incubus . . . thus advis'd.
> > Set women in his eye and in his walk,
> Among daughters of men the fairest found; . . .
> Such object hath the power to soft'n and tame
> Severest temper, smooth the rugged'st brow,
> Enerve, and with voluptuous hope dissolve. . . .
> > To whom quick answer Satan thus return'd.
> Belial, in much uneven scale thou weigh'st
> All others by thyself. (2. 150-74.)

Jesus, who had already refused the satisfaction of simple hunger, was not likely to fall prey to lower appetites. In Biblical phrase, he had said:

> Think'st thou such force in Bread? is it not
> > written . . .
> Man lives not by Bread only, but each Word
> Proceeding from the mouth of God? (1. 347-50.)

The interpretation later given to this denial of hunger turns on the Platonic opposition of body and soul:

> Though hunger still remain: so it remain
> Without this body's wasting, I content me, . . .
> Nor mind it, fed with better thoughts that feed
> Mee hung'ring more to do my Fathers will. (2. 255-9.)

If Satan hopes to trap Jesus through 'Lawful desires of Nature,' he is defeated before he starts. He has been Platonist enough, as distinguished from Belial, to recognize that unnecessary and ignoble pleasures tempt only the most degraded; he is also Platonist enough to see that pleasures of sight and smell are more likely to win a noble mind than the pleasure of taste alone. The banquet he provides is therefore not for the mere gourmand, but for the aesthete. But Jesus replies to the whole offer:

> Thy pompous Delicacies I contemn. (2. 390.)

Satan has offered him all at once the most pleasant satisfaction for all honorable desires, but offered them in opposition to better goods. And Satan recognizes which of the goods Jesus has spurned, and which of the Platonic virtues he has demonstrated, observing:

> Thy temperance invincible besides,
> For no allurement yields to appetite. (2. 408-9.)

The temptation of pleasure comes again in connection with other goods, but still without the one good which makes the virtue of every other; and Jesus again rejects the lure:

> Nor doth this grandeur and majestic show
> Of luxury, though call'd magnificence,
> More than of arms before, allure mine eye,
> Much less my mind. (4. 110-3.)

And like Plato on the Syracusans, he condemns the people

> grown . . .
> Luxurious by thir wealth, and greedier still,
> And from the daily Scene effeminate. (4. 141-3.)

To those who set pleasure highest in the scale of goods Milton made one constant answer, the query in which Jesus speaks his utter scorn of the vulgar concern with the stomach:

> And with my hunger what hast thou to do? (2. 389.)

Neither Milton nor the Jesus of his *Paradise Regained* denies the need or the pleasure that would attend its satisfaction, but there are more important principles of choice than the impulse of desire. The happy life will include satisfaction for every need; Jesus will banquet, when the temptations are over, on 'Celestial Food, Divine, Ambrosial,' will enjoy what is due to palate, eye, and ear—but not until he has put last things last. And pleasure is last in Milton's as in Plato's scale.

WEALTH

In the *Republic* Socrates ranks wealth as an object of pursuit intermediate between sensual pleasure and power. Like other goods popularly thought to be the means to happiness, wealth is itself neither good nor bad; but the undue importance usually given to it vulgarizes the soul, and its frequent use for a life of self-indulgence makes it a source of corruption. Of these principles Plato is convinced throughout the Dialogues. The good man will neither need nor desire, and is therefore not likely to obtain, great riches; while to the unjust man they are a positive evil, aiding him to accomplish his self-perversion. Since even honest gain if too zealously pursued taints the soul, and since the zealous pursuit of gain often leads to dishonesty, riches can hardly occupy the man bent on finding happiness. Yet Plato holds no ascetic ideal of poverty, but freely admits the deliberalizing effects of extreme want. The proper state is one of limited needs duly satisfied in order that a man may proceed to his proper tasks. And hence the careful regulations of wealth in the *Laws,* and the communism imposed upon the ruling class in the *Republic.* Let men be freed from the cares of poverty, and secured against the vices of luxury, thinks Plato, and they may then direct their attention to more humane concerns. He is thus at one with Ruskin in distinguishing between wealth and 'illth,' but even more decisively rejects popular notions of value.

For both, the test is usefulness for human good; but for Plato material prosperity cannot ever be of real benefit, and as it is far more likely to divert men from what is really beneficial, wealth must be spurned in the search for happiness.[3]

Like most high-minded men, Milton feels a similar scorn for the popular interest in money-making. If there is little that is distinctively Platonic in this feeling, still his agreement with Plato is complete. He dwells very little on the question of riches, thinking it a vulgar concern, and quickly turns his attention to more important matters. In an early letter, he compliments Thomas Young on being able to

reign peacefully over [his] little estate, and, despising fortune, triumph over wealth, ambition, pomp, luxury, and all that common men admire and gape at. (Tillyard, p. 9.)

The distinction between what the herd admires and the wise man's interest is repeated in *Ad Patrem:*

Go, gather wealth, fool, whoever you are, that prefer the ancient treasures of Austria, and of the Peruvian realms. But what more than learning could my father have given, or Jove himself had he given all but heaven? (Mac Kellar, p. 149.)

Here Milton believes, like Plato, that exaggerated interest in money is a perversion of the natural yearning for good, and opposed to the desire for knowledge.

In the anti-Prelatical writings, where Milton turns his attention to the economy of the Church, he necessarily becomes more concerned with the effects of wealth and its pursuit. And now his judgments become more recognizably Platonic. We need not repeat in detail his accusations against a money-loving clergy; a passage from the *Apology for Smectymnuus* will show their doctrinal basis:

Therefore must the ministers of Christ not be over-rich or

---

[2] See especially *Republic* 8. 549-55; *Laws* 5. 742-4.

-great in the world, because their calling is spiritual, not secular; because they have a special warfare, which is not to be entangled with many impediments, . . . and lastly because a middle estate is most proper to the office of teaching. (3. 364.)

Milton demands of the clergy what Plato demanded of his philosopher-kings: both groups, dedicated to a life of service, are to be freed from worldly concerns, not by embracing the life of poverty, but by being maintained in a 'middle estate,' untroubled by need, and unimpeded by wealth.

In *Eikonoclastes,* Milton restates the effect of wealth upon the clergy:

When ministers came to have lands, houses, farms, coaches, horses, and the like lumber, then religion brought forth riches in the Church, and the daughter devoured the mother. (5. 233.)

Thenceforth and with increasing emphasis, he connects wealth with the vices of luxury as surely as Plato held that a plutocracy was but one short step from the pleasure-seeking life of a democracy. In his first *Defensio,* he traces the corruption of the Church:

Afterwards, the Church, which he [Constantine] had vastly enriched, began to fall in love with offices, absolute rule, and secular power, and then the Christian religion went to wrack. First luxury and sloth, and then a crew of all the heresies and vices, as if their dungeons had been set open from behind, trooped over into the Church; thereupon envy, hatred, and discord overflowed everywhere, and at last they . . . were as much at variance and strife as the bitterest enemies. (7. 257-9.)

Finally, the *Means to Remove Hirelings* treats at length of the need to exorcise from the Church every last taint of acquisitiveness by prohibiting regular pay to ministers. Much in the vein of Plato's remarks on the Sophists who taught for money, Milton writes:

The corruption of teachers, most commonly the effect of

hire, is the very bane of truth in them who are so corrupted. (6. 46.)

Even more like the Platonic notion that philosophers must rule, and not for salary, is the assertion to Parliament:

Till which grievances be removed, and religion set free from the monopoly of hirelings, I dare affirm that no model whatsoever of a commonwealth will prove successful or undisturbed. (6. 45.)

The phrasing echoes the famous 'great wave' of the *Republic* 5. 473:

Unless philosophers bear kingly rule in cities, or those who are now called kings and princes become genuine and adequate philosophers, and political power and philosophy are brought together, . . . there will be no respite from evil, my dear Glaucon, for cities, nor, I fancy, for humanity.

And Milton echoes the conviction of Plato that from wealth flows ill, not good, that the just man, group, or nation will not be concerned with acquiring riches, and that riches could be useful to none but the just. Very close indeed to the account of civic degeneration in the *Republic* are these words from *Eikonoclastes:*

For wealth and plenty in a land where justice reigns not is no argument of a flourishing State, but of a nearness rather to ruin or commotion. (5. 154.)

The experience of cupidity in Church and State apparently taught Milton how prevalent and vicious was the money-hunting that he had once dismissed as merely perverse, for in his later poetry wealth receives more explicit treatment, and denunciation. Mammon he describes in *Paradise Lost* as

> the least erected Spirit that fell
> From heav'n, for ev'n in heav'n his looks
> and thoughts

> Were always downward bent, admiring more
> The riches of Heav'n's pavement, trodd'n Gold,
> Than aught divine or holy else enjoy'd
> In vision beatific. (1. 679-84.)

The principle of judgment is Platonic: he who concentrates upon the lesser good forgets the highest. And the admonition that follows shows how completely Milton had come to associate wealth with corruption:

> Let none admire
> That riches grow in Hell; that soil may best
> Deserve the precious bane. (1. 690-2.)

Later in the poem Michael comments on a part of the historical panorama he is presenting:

> For a while
> In mean estate live moderate, till grown
> In wealth and multitude, factious they grow. (12. 350-2.)

We are reminded of the change recounted in the *Republic* (2. 372-4) from the primitive State with its simple needs to the luxurious 'State at fever-heat' in which a military class is first required.

For Milton's most explicit judgment of wealth, as of every other good, we must turn to *Paradise Regained*. There Satan on finding that Jesus can resist the life of pleasure tries him with the temptation that Plato had thought a degree less base. Associating wealth with the power to which it may be a means, he argues:

> Great acts require great means of enterprise. . . .
> Money brings Honour, Friends, Conquest, and Realms. . . .
> Therefore, if at great things thou wouldst arrive,
> Get Riches first, get Wealth, and Treasure heap,
> Not difficult, if thou hearken to me,
> Riches are mine, Fortune is in my hand;
> They whom I favour thrive in wealth amain,
> While Virtue, Valour, Wisdom sit in want.

Jesus at once answers:

> Yet wealth without these three is impotent,
> To gain dominion or to keep it gain'd,
> Witness those ancient Empires of the Earth,
> In highth of all thir flowing wealth dissolv'd;
> But men endu'd with these have oft attain'd
> In lowest poverty to highest deeds. . . .
> Extol not Riches then, the toil of Fools,
> The wise man's cumbrance if not snare, more apt
> To slacken Virtue, and abate her edge,
> Than prompt her to do aught may merit praise. (2. 412-56.)

His reply is thoroughly Platonic: 'Virtue, Valour, Wisdom' are the true necessities; without them wealth causes its own ruin. So Socrates had argued:

> The excess of wealth, and the neglect of all else but money-making, destroyed oligarchy. (*Rep.* 8. 562.)

Further, against the many who suppose wealth to be the object of the State, Plato's second lawgiver, the Athenian, asserted:

> I can never concede . . . that a rich man is truly happy unless he is also a good man; but that one who is exceptionally good should be exceptionally wealthy too is a mere impossibility. (*Laws* 5. 743 a.)

Ultimately each man must choose among the so-called goods, not only as one surpasses another, but as pursuit of one hinders pursuit of another. With Milton as with Plato there can be no question between wealth and virtue, and Plato's sentence will suffice to state the final judgment both make:

> Purchase for purchase, I shall have made a better bargain in a better cause, if I choose to get rectitude for my soul rather than wealth for my pocket. (*Laws* 11. 913.)

If Plato and Milton are not alone in this belief, still we

do well to remember that some, even among philosophers, have not shared it. Milton at least was conscious of another opinion on the subject, for in *Paradise Regained* he has Jesus remark of one school of thought:

> Others in virtue plac'd felicity,
> But virtue join'd with riches and long life. (4. 297-8.)

The others are clearly of the Peripatetic school, repeating the words of Aristotle:

> He is happy who is active in accordance with complete virtue and is sufficiently equipped with external goods, not for some chance period but throughout a complete life. (*Eth. Nic.* 1. 10. 1101a.)

Plato alone among ancient philosophers placed felicity in a virtue neither ascetic like that of the Stoics nor dependent upon good fortune like that of the Peripatetics, but a virtue which of itself would bring all lesser goods by its very independence of them. When Jesus, at the end of his trials, becomes 'heir of both worlds,' gaining wealth far beyond Satan's most lavish offer, Milton surely has it in mind to demonstrate the Biblical maxim of Matthew 6. 33: 'But seek ye first the kingdom of God, and his righteousness; and all these things shall be added unto you.' But he might also take the reward as proof of the Platonic doctrine:

> For surely the gods do not neglect him who will bestir himself to become just. . . . Then at the hands of gods the just man will get some such prizes as these. . . . At the end of every action and partnership, and at the end of life, they [the just] win a good report and carry off prizes at men's hand. (*Rep.* 10. 613.)

The principle, whether taken from the Bible or from Plato, is the same; and Milton, a Christian Platonist, holds it firmly. Wealth, far from being the chief good or even its necessary support, is a hindrance to man's true object; and only when scorned for itself, can it be appropriately and in due measure added to adorn the happiness which must be sought elsewhere.

FAME

Milton gives to 'fame' much the same meaning and value as Plato gives to τιμή; both occasionally use other words for the concept.[4] By derivation, 'fame' simply means report, and τιμή worth; ordinarily, however, both words signify high esteem, one of the goods chiefly desired by mankind. In Plato's scheme this desire is next to the highest, which is of wisdom and virtue. Indeed, the yearning for honor is the least perverted expression of a universal longing for eternal happiness, the root of every desire. Those who are dominated by love of τιμή are the ambitious, the φιλότιμοι, ranking in worth just below the best men who control this love by a higher, the φιλόσοφοι. Still, ambition itself can control lower appetites, and not the desire but its dominion over the higher love is wrong; for all men want what the φιλότιμοι want, not only as all want everlasting happiness, which these think to obtain by honor, but as all want a fair reputation. The great difference is that the φιλόσοφος wishes to deserve esteem; the φιλότιμος primarily regards the esteem, whether or not it is duly earned. In consequence, while to the lover of wisdom only the opinion of wise and good men is important, the lover of honor cares little about the source of his praise. And hence the philosopher desires and secures a truer and more perfect honor than he who seeks honor alone. True fame lies not simply in high esteem, but in the merited esteem of good judges, or even in merit whether it is recognized or not. In this last sense of τιμή, the Athenian of the *Laws* can affirm:

Honor, I take it, is a thing divinely good, and can be conferred by nothing that is evil. (*Laws* 5. 727 a.)

[4] See Ast, *Lexicon Platonicum* under δόξα and φήμη as well as τιμή. The various terms used by Milton appear in the present section.

This conception of τιμή reappears in every detail in Milton's treatment of fame. To what extent Milton himself shared the universal longing for good repute the autobiographical portions of his verse and prose amply reveal. Commentators have exaggerated his desire as idiosyncratic; Milton recognized it as human, in himself because in all mankind. As early as the year 1632 or 1633, he admitted the existence of

a desire of honor and repute and immortal fame seated in the breast of every true scholar. (12. 324.)

The fame desired is immortal, as Plato held, and the men to whom the desire is imputed are a class better than most.

But while still an undergraduate at Christ's College Milton had recognized an even more desirable state:

To have no thought of glory when we do well is above all glory. (Tillyard, pp. 117-8.)

The higher spirits are more tempted by praise, while the highest overcome the temptation. Because Milton keenly feels this superiority, he denies with emphasis the charge of writing for renown:

But I was not eager for fame, who is slow of pace; indeed, if the fit opportunity had not been given me, even these things would never have seen the light; little concerned, though others were ignorant that I knew what I did. It was not the fame of every thing that I was waiting for, but the opportunity. (8. 113.)

Like Plato, he thus comes to have what seems a varying, but is in fact a steady, view of honor. The esteem won from the ignorant many becomes despicable in *Paradise Lost:*

Thus Fame shall be achiev'd, renown on Earth,
And what most merits fame in silence hid. (11. 698-9.)

They who care for such renown, the φιλότιμοι at their worst, eventually come to wish, as Nimrod wished, simply to

> get themselves a name, lest far disperst
> In foreign Lands thir memory be lost,
> Regardless whether good or evil fame. (12. 45-7.)

But as there is worthless praise, the ignorant acclaim of undeserving men, there is also a glory more properly desirable, the deserved regard of the judicious; and this praise Milton could wish to have.

In his first Academic Exercise at Cambridge he was already aware that his audience must be few if they were to be fit:

> The approval of these, few though they be, is more precious to me than that of the countless hosts of the ignorant, who lack all intelligence, reasoning power, and sound judgment. (Tillyard, pp. 53-4.)

He asks in the *Reason of Church-Government* to be 'heard only, if it might be, by the elegant and learned reader' (3. 234)—because here fitness to judge depends upon a knowledge comparable to the learnedness of the subject. But where erudition and elegance are not demanded by the occasion, Milton's fit audience is composed of the morally even more than of the intellectually eminent. In 1659, presumably at the time when he was composing *Paradise Lost,* he wrote to Jean Labadie:

> It is my conviction that the only real fame I can claim is the good opinion held of me by good men. (Tillyard, p. 47.)

The sentence is an accurate condensation of Plato's scattered remarks on τιμή.

From this distinction between proper and improper judges, it is but a step to the notion that truest fame is the opinion of the truest judge, God. Here a Christian element enters the concept which thus far exactly reproduces that of Plato, but only the character of the judge alters, not the character of the judgment; for Plato, like Milton, held the final decision on human worth to be beyond human wisdom, and the true honor divine. Thus in *Comus*, the glory awarded is Plato's own notion of τιμή with nothing supra-Platonic in the lines but the word 'faith':

> Heav'n hath timely tri'd their youth,
> Their faith, their patience, and their truth.
> And sent them here through hard assays
> With a crown of deathless Praise. (969-72.)

Again the eloquent passage in *Lycidas* contains no element opposed to Plato's view. The 'Dorick' singer begins:

> Alas! What boots it with uncessant care
> To tend the homely slighted Shepherd's trade,
> And strictly meditate the thankless Muse?
> Were it not better done as others use,
> To sport with Amaryllis in the shade,
> Or with the tangles of Neaera's hair?
> Fame is the spur that the clear spirit doth raise
> (That last infirmity of Noble mind)
> To scorn delights, and live laborious days.

According to Plato also, the desire of fame can stir men to unwonted toil. Wise Diotima explains the impulse, and specifically names poets among those most affected by it:

Marvel not then at the love which all men have of their off-spring; for that universal love and interest is for the sake of immortality. . . . Of that, Socrates, you may be assured;—think only of the ambition of men, and you will wonder at the sense-lessness of their ways, unless you consider how they are stirred by the love of an immortality of fame. They are ready to run all risks, greater far than they would have run for their children, and to spend money and undergo any sort of toil, and even to die, for the sake of leaving behind them a name which shall be eternal. . . . I am persuaded that all men do all things, and the better they are the more they do them, in hope of the glorious fame of immortal virtue; for they desire the immortal.

89

Those who are pregnant in the body only, betake themselves to women and beget children—this is the character of their love; their offspring, as they hope, will preserve their memory and give them the blessedness and immortality which they desire in the future. But souls which are pregnant—for there certainly are men who are more creative in their souls than in their bodies—conceive that which is proper for the soul to conceive or contain. And what are these conceptions?—wisdom and virtue in general. And such creatures are poets and all artists who are deserving of the name inventor. (*Symposium* 208-9.)

Ambition can thus cast out every lower desire as Socrates affirms in the *Republic* (9. 581) and elsewhere. And still the hope of praise is an infirmity, though the last since least erroneous: the φιλότιμος is just below the φιλόσοφος, since the nobler mind is naturally more susceptible to the error nearest the true way. (Cf. *Phaedrus* 256 and *Republic* 6. 491-2.) But the desire, even when of merit as well as of acclaim, is still in error, as life itself, the test of ethical truth, demonstrates:

> But the fair Guerdon when we hope to find,
> And think to burst out into sudden blaze,
> Comes the blind Fury with th' abhorred shears,
> And slits the thin-spun life.

Why, then, the toil of virtue if the reward is uncertain, the singer asks, much as Glaucon and Adeimantus had asked of Socrates (*Rep.* 2. 358-68); and he receives a Socratic answer:

> Fame is no plant that grows on mortal soil,
> Nor in the glistering foil
> Set off to th' world, nor in broad rumour lies,
> But lives and spreads aloft by those pure eyes,
> And perfet witness of all judging Jove;
> As He pronounces lastly on each deed,
> Of so much fame in Heav'n expect thy meed.

Only the 'perfect witness' can pronounce true praise or blame, the everlasting honor is in the deed itself, recognition is therefore desirable and meaningful only from the knowing judge, and he will assuredly grant it.

Compare this concept of fame with that of others, and its Platonism shows clear. Virgil's notion, for example, which Milton, following Downham, carefully dissected in his *Logic* (11. 274-8), is merely 'broad rumour,' here rejected as inadequate. Closer to Milton's view is the discussion in Cicero's *Dream of Scipio;* but even that passage, though in the Academic strain, resembles Milton's less completely than the scattered reflections of Plato. Plato and Milton, unlike Cicero and Virgil, grant that the human need for recognition is an integral part of the desire for happiness and that every human need if kept in due proportion can be itself right and rightly satisfied. Τιμή is not to be discarded because virtue is more desirable, but rather to be transmuted into the image of virtue, to lose its infirmity and become the strength and solace of the noble mind. When the various desires follow truth, says Plato, they each enjoy 'the truest pleasures that they are capable of receiving' (*Rep.* 9. 586-7). Wherefore the Athenian Stranger maintains:

> When I bid men honor their own souls next to the gods, our sovereign lords, and the powers under them, the counsel I give is right. Yet not a man of us, I may say, honors his soul aright, though he dreams he does. Honor, I take it, is a thing divinely good, and can be conferred by nothing that is evil. . . . Honor, we hold, is, in sum, to follow after what is better, and for what is worse but may be amended, e'en to make it good as best may be. (*Laws* 5. 727-8.)

Worth and honor are thus ultimately identical since they are identical with the happiness of man. The proper distinction is between true and false notions of honor. If there is a difference between the views of Milton and Plato, it is the higher importance in Milton of the 'perfet witness,' in Plato of the inner consciousness of worth.

Paradise Regained repeats every element of the doctrine in *Lycidas*, but more fully and with a more complete opposition of heavenly to earthly glory. As the treatment is enlarged, Milton's shift of emphasis becomes clearer, while his essential agreement with Plato remains. From the first, Jesus desires high achievements. He recollects how, as a boy,

> my Spirit aspir'd, victorious deeds
> Flam'd in my heart, heroic acts. (1. 215-6.)

And his mother encouraged him, even as Plato or Milton would:

> High are thy thoughts
> O Son, but nourish them and let them soar
> To what highth sacred virtue and true worth
> Can raise them, though above example high. (1. 229-32.)

Satan immediately recognizes the 'timocratic' character in Jesus:

> But he whom we attempt is wiser far
> Than Solomon, of more exalted mind,
> Made and set wholly on the accomplishment
> Of greatest things. (2. 205-8.)

Knowing this, Satan rejects the advice of Belial that he tempt Jesus with sensual pleasures, and counters:

> With manlier objects we must try
> His constancy, with such as have more shew
> Of worth, of honour, glory, and popular praise. (2. 226-8.)

Many a philosophical nature has been deluded by Satan's very first argument:

> All thy heart is set on high designs,

High actions; but wherewith to be achiev'd?
Great acts require great means of enterprise. (2. 410-2.)

History records their names and Plato explains their fall from the first high purpose.

Then consider how many and how great are the causes of destruction to those rare souls. . . . One you will be extremely surprised to hear. Each of those very qualities which we praised as belonging to the philosophic nature destroys the soul possessing them and draws it away from philosophy—I mean courage, temperance, and the rest. . . . Or do you fancy that great crimes and unmixed wickedness come from a feeble nature and not rather from a noble nature ruined by education? (*Rep.* 6. 491.)

Knowing his own powers, knowing what such powers can win, Jesus would seem fair prey to the next of Satan's arguments for fame:

These God-like Virtues wherefore dost thou hide?
Affecting private life, or more obscure
In savage Wilderness, wherefore deprive
All Earth her wonder at thy acts, thyself
The fame and glory, glory the reward
That sole excites to high attempts the flame
Of most erected Spirits, most temper'd pure
Aetherial, who all pleasures else despise,
All treasures and all gain esteem as dross,
And dignities and powers all but the highest. (3. 21-30.)

Ever the sophist, Satan has mixed his little lie into the truth. 'Fame *is* the spur,' but not the sole one. It does excite the 'noble mind,' but not the '*most* erected.' The ambitious do 'scorn delights,' but so do others. Jesus refutes this sophistry by first distinguishing between the two kinds of fame:

What is glory, but the blaze of fame,

93

The people's praise, if always praise unmixt?
And what the people but a herd confus'd,
A miscellaneous rabble, who extol
Things vulgar, and well weigh'd, scarce worth
        the praise?
They praise and they admire they know not what;
And know not whom, but as one leads the other;
And what delight to be by such extoll'd,
To live upon thir tongues and be thir talk,
Of whom to be disprais'd were no small praise?
His lot who dares be singularly good.
Th' intelligent among them and the wise
Are few, and glory scarce of few is rais'd. (3. 47-59.)

This is what Socrates had repeated in the Dialogues, and the Athenian of the *Laws* had said. The confused opinion of the rabble is not fame, while the judicious are too few to grant renown. Only one right hope of esteem can remain:

This is true glory and renown, when God
Looking on the Earth, with approbation marks
The just man, and divulges him through Heaven
To all his Angels, who with true applause
Recount his praises. (3. 60-4.)

Again Milton has shifted from the Platonic emphasis on inner merit to the Christian emphasis on heavenly glory. But 'the just man' who wins 'true glory and renown' is Plato's. Milton gives us assurance on this point: the first illustration of this true glory is Biblical Job, but the second is Socrates,

Poor Socrates (who next more memorable?)
By what he taught and suffer'd for so doing,
For truth's sake suffering death unjust, lives now
Equal in fame to proudest Conquerors. (3. 96-9.)

Plato was right. Remember that, in discussing how the

philosophical nature deteriorates into the ambitious, he had made Socrates prefigure his own martyrdom; the last inducement against philosophical pursuits was the practical argument of 'dishonor, fines, and death' (*Rep.* 6. 492). And Socrates ended the discussion by asserting that the philosophical nature, if it is to be saved at all, must be 'saved by the power of God.' Jesus is the philosopher saved by divine power, as Job and Socrates were saved for pursuit of the real praise. The question and answer to Satan are:

> Shall I seek glory then, as vain men seek
> Oft not deserv'd? I seek not mine, but his
> Who sent me, and thereby witness whence I am. (3. 106-8.)

Again the Christian change is struck in Plato's tune, and yet once more repeated:

> Yet so much bounty is in God, such grace,
> That who advance his glory, not thir own,
> Them he himself to glory will advance. (3. 142-4.)

Jesus, however, apparently thinks Socrates among those who sought to advance the glory of God; and Milton consequently would seem to make no distinction between Plato's insistence on inner worth and his own insistence on the heavenly reward of worth.

At any rate, the semi-Platonic sophistry of the tempter is refuted by the wholly Platonic philosophy of Jesus. Whether or not a supra-Platonic line completes the argument, it does complete the adventure, for Milton is not content to leave his philosopher with the τιμή of unregarded merit, but at the last gives him the express honor of hearing an angelic choir sing:

> Queller of Satan, on thy *glorious* work
> Now enter, and begin to save mankind.
> > (4. 634-5, italics mine.)

PLATONIC DOCTRINES CITED BY MILTON
ETHICS

Plato heads the list of 'moral works' to be studied in an academy. *Of Ed.* (4. 284.)

Love

Alcibiades' love of Socrates is associated with seeking the other half of one's soul. *Eleg.* 4. 23-4.

Socratic doctrine taught Milton to reject the yoke of desire. *Eleg.* 7, Postscript.

Milton learned the doctrine of true love from Plato and Xenophon. *Ap. Smect.* (3. 305.)

The myth of love's birth in the *Symposium* agrees with the Mosaic account. *D.D.D.* (3. 398.)

The myth of Aristophanes in the *Symposium* erroneously suggests that man and woman are equal. *Tetrach.* (4. 76.)

Knowledge

Socratic ignorance is coupled with the caution of the sceptics. *Prolus.* 7 (12. 280.)

The learned conferences of Plato would be worth hearing. *Prolus.* 7 (12. 262-4.)

The Sophists, who taught for hire, were refuted by the Socratics. *Church-Gov.* (3. 202.)

Socrates in the Dialogues often refutes Sophists. *Ap. Smect.* (3. 293-4.)

Those who could not refute Socrates blamed his persuasive power. *Tetrach.* (4. 70.)

Socrates died for the sake of truth. *P.R.* 3. 96-9.

Socrates rightly professed ignorance, and was therefore the wisest of the heathen. *P.R.* 4. 293-4.

Virtue

Every man has a guiding genius in his conscience. *Ap. Smect.* (3. 318.)

Admonition and reproof purify the soul according to Plato. *Church-Gov.* (3. 264.)

Both destiny and will must combine to make men virtuous according to Academic doctrine. *D.D.D.* (3. 441.)

Men err involuntarily, as Plato says in *Protagoras* and elsewhere. *D.D.D.* (3. 464.)

Fame

Socrates won true fame through his virtue. *P.R.* 3. 96-9.

Amusement

Socrates often indulged in jests. *Prolus.* 6 (12. 218, 238.)

Plato's Dialogues are like mimes, and Plato enjoyed the humor of mimes. *Ap. Smect.* (3. 293-4.)

There is much jesting in the Dialogues. *Pro Se Def.* (9. 176, 180-2.)

Plato indulged in fables and 'smooth conceits.' *P.R.* 4. 295.

POLITICS

Plato, the 'wisest of the heathen,' is an authority on law. *Church-Gov.* (3. 181-2.)

The Ideal State

Plato rightly thought slight changes in custom a danger to the State. To Buommattei (12. 32.)

Plato's mythical island in *Critias* teaches us better notions of government. *Ap. Smect.* (3. 294.)

The censorship of the *Republic* is unnecessarily severe. *Tetrach.* (4. 157-8.)

The presentation of Utopian states as in the *Republic* is useless, and the censorship there favored is erroneous. *Areop.* (4. 316-7.)

Plato's 'laws of virtuous education' are the true safeguard of his ideal State. *Areop.* (4. 318.)

Law

Laws should have an explanatory preface, as Plato says in the *Laws*. *Church-Gov.* (3. 181-2.)

According to the *Laws* 4, there should be no contradictory statutes. *D.D.D.* (3. 458-9.)

Law and nature really agree, as Socrates shows in *Gorgias*. *D.D.D.* (3. 500-1.)

The Ruler

According to Plato and others the good of the State constitutes the good of the king. *Of Ref.* (3. 39.)

Plato calls magistrates the servants of the Law in the *Laws* and the Eighth *Epistle*. *Def.* (7. 158, 166-8, 304-6.)

Plato, one of the wisest men, praised Lycurgus for limiting the king's power. *Def.* (7. 348-50.)

Education

Plato's system of education is the proper basis of his ideal State. *Areop.* (4. 318.)

'Socratic discourses' are to be used as books on educational theory in the proposed academies. *Of Ed.* (4. 281.)

The proposed academy is like that of Plato, and should prevent defects in the State. *Of Ed.* (4. 287.)

Marriage

In the *Laws* 6, Plato affirmed that offspring were desirable, and related the institution of marriage to the good of the State. *Tetrach.* (4. 81.)

Liberty

Plato recommended the works of Aristophanes, although these seem to be the kind he would have censored. *Areop.* (4. 299.)

In the Eighth *Epistle,* Plato advocated a just mixture of law and liberty. *Def.* (7. 350.)

THEORIES OF ART

Plato was provided with 'grave Doric' arts to substitute for those he banned from the *Republic. Areop.* (4. 317.)

Poetry

The myth in *Phaedrus* has given Milton an image of his own poetic hopes. To Diodati (12. 26.)

Rhetoric

Rhetoric is to be taught from the 'rule of Plato' and others. *Of Ed.* (4. 286.)

For the proper use of jests, see *Ethics: Amusement.*

Music

Plato rightly followed Pythagoras in maintaining the doctrine of the harmony of the spheres. *Prolus.* 2 (12. 150.)

METAPHYSICS

Plato is a most skilful interpreter of nature. *Prolus.* 2 (12. 150.)

The Cosmos

Milton will 'unsphere' Plato to learn where the souls of the dead dwell. *Il Pens.* 87-96.

The Ideas

Aristotle looks for the Platonic Idea in the wrong way. *Idea Plat.*

Milton seeks the Idea of the Beautiful described in *Phaedrus.* To Diodati (12. 26.)

CHAPTER V

The Good Life: Knowledge

LIKE Plato, Milton rejects pleasure, wealth, and power with its attendant fame, as the chief means to happiness. Only one good remains in the Platonic scheme, knowledge or wisdom, between which terms Plato makes little distinction. Philosophy is the love of the rational element of the soul; its object, truth, becomes knowledge in possession and wisdom in action. For Plato wisdom as the function or virtue is always the immediate effect of knowledge, which is the form of truth in the mind. As such, knowledge is the ultimate goal of all men's striving, if they but knew it; for the happiness universally sought is eternal possession of the good, and the good by its very nature can be possessed only by being known. Further, knowledge by producing wisdom produces all virtue—justice, fortitude, and temperance being so many aspects of the single habit of choice that results from vision of truth. And hence philosophy is the real pursuit of happiness, and knowledge the *summum bonum*.

Not every kind of knowledge, however. According to *Charmides* 174, 'the crown of happiness' is bestowed by the 'science of good and evil.' The Idea of the Good, mystically presented in the *Republic* as an object of knowledge higher than justice and the other virtues, means at one time the source of all truth imaginatively seen in its unity, at another the ethical concept of perfect virtue. In general, throughout the Dialogues, ethical knowledge is the highest, the ultimate truth, and every other learning is subordinated as a tool of this science or a discipline preparatory to it. Since ethics and politics are for Plato merely the individual and social aspects of a single body of principles, the architectonic science of the good appears now as the 'kingly art, having supreme authority' (as in *Euthydemus* 291), now as the guide of personal life.

For this reason the kings of the *Republic* are to be philosophers, and the guardians of the *Laws* are to have special instruction in the 'one idea' which is the single principle in virtue and the good, and, even more important, a training in theology not required of most citizens. (See the *Laws* 12. 965-6.) In Plato's thought, as seldom outside of some Christian writings, knowledge of God, of truth, and of the good become one and inseparable. And because he regards the whole of human life as a unit, and the guiding of it to proper ends as a single task, he rigorously subordinates every other activity, intellectual or productive, to the principal activity, and every other knowledge, of theory or craft, to the architectonic knowledge of philosophy.

And hence the seeming inconsistency of various passages in the Dialogues. At one time natural science is derided as well-nigh useless, but at another receives remarkably thorough attention. Here poets are banished from the Republic, there taken as the 'fathers to us of all knowledge.' But however the particular judgment varies with the occasion, a constant principle remains: Keep first things and the knowledge of them first. Where a subordinate learning impedes, dispense with it; where it can be the instrument of a higher, retain it. There is much mockery of useless knowledge in the Dialogues, but no knowledge is ever condemned in itself; it is useless when given undue importance or employed for a wrong end. Only one kind of knowledge may exist for its own sake, and that is the kind that never professes to: the ethical knowledge represented as the pursuit of Socrates, and figured in the various dialogues as the Absolute Beauty, the Good, or the 'one idea' in all the virtues.

True knowledge, and Plato refuses to call any other sort knowledge at all, is thus the chief good, intellectually as it satisfies the desire of reason for truth, ethically since it corresponds to and produces the ruling virtue of the soul, and politically because in application to the social life of man it begets the highest order of civilization. If Aristotle disliked Plato's 'Universal Good' because it could mean many things, Plato apparently liked it for that very reason: the Idea of the Good can unite in symbol all the varied aspects of the happiness which man attains through knowledge.

With Milton the highest good for man is a synthesis of elements even more diverse than entered into the concept of Plato, but again unified, as was Plato's by a single principle. The principle is no longer Platonic, but Plato took Milton far on his way toward a distinctively Christian goal for men. He had only to cap the Platonic ideal in order to change the highest good from the philosophical life praised in the Dialogues to the 'more abundant' life of Christianity. Augustine had said of the Platonists, in *The City of God* (8.5), '*Nulli nobis quam isti proprius accesserunt.*' And Ficino had written to his fellow-Platonist, Giovanni Pico della Mirandola: '*Philosophica ingenia ad Christum perveniunt per Platonem.*' Milton felt the same. We find in his ethic nothing subtracted from Plato's, but only something added.

For Milton, as in the Dialogues, knowledge far surpasses the other goals men set themselves, as more fully satisfactory to the whole of human nature. The glorification of philosophy in his Cambridge exercises already resembles Plato's, especially the Seventh in Defense of Knowledge, with its rejection of Ignorance as 'the life of a beast.' The wise lady of the *Symposium* may have taught the matter for his argument:

God would indeed seem to have endowed us to no purpose, or even to our distress, with this soul which is capable and indeed insatiably desirous of the highest wisdom, if he had not intended us to strive with all our might toward the lofty understanding of those things, for which he had at our creation instilled so great a longing into the human mind. (Tillyard, pp. 107-8.)

And even beyond satisfying the mind, knowledge provides the key to happiness, individual and social:

If then Learning is our guide and leader in the search after happiness, if it is ordained and approved by almighty God, and most conformable to His glory, surely it cannot but bring the greatest blessings upon those who follow after it. . . .

And indeed a single household, even a single individual, endowed with the gifts of Art and Wisdom, may often prove to be a great gift of God, and sufficient to lead a whole State to righteousness. (*Ibid.*, pp. 108-9.)

And hence in the letter to Gill, July 2, 1628, the disapproval of those who

take their flight to theology before ever they are fledged, almost untrained and uninitiated in literature and philosophy alike. (P. 8.)

These are the 'blind mouths' of *Lycidas,* who

> scarce themselves know how to hold
> A Sheep-hook, or have learn'd aught else the least
> That to the faithful Herdman's art belongs!

With Milton, the charge of ignorance is as damning as with Plato.

Similarly, in defending knowledge against the groundless accusations of the uninitiate, they are at one. As the younger brother in *Comus* puts it:

> How charming is divine Philosophy!
> Not harsh and crabbed as dull fools suppose,
> But musical as is Apollo's lute,
> And a perpetual feast of nectar'd sweets,
> Where no crude surfeit reigns. (475-80.)

The last phrase looks forward to Adam's speech of grati-
tude for the instruction Raphael has given him:

> [Fruits] satiate, and soon fill,
> Though pleasant, but thy words with Grace Divine
> Imbu'd, bring to thir sweetness no satiety. (8. 214-6.)

Thus Plato had opposed the pleasures of learning to those
of sense, and Milton twice adopts the opposition in order to
magnify knowledge in the scale of human good.

Milton, who took 'intent study' as his 'portion in this life,'
spoke of the joy he himself felt in 'beholding the bright
countenance of truth in the quiet and still air of delightful
studies' (*Church-Gov.* 3. 241). To be sure, men innumerable have found learning a delight, and if this were the
whole or even a separable aspect of Milton's theory, we
should hardly call it Platonic. But in Milton and Plato we
find the same emphasis on the charm of study coupled with
the same critical scrutiny of its use. Both insist on the constant devotion of subordinate learnings to a higher end, and
reserve for that end the term 'knowledge.' The true knowledge satisfies reason, promotes virtue, and serves the common weal. Hear Milton, then, on false learning:

> Finally, the supreme result of all this earnest labor is to
> make you a more finished fool and cleverer contriver of con-
> ceits, and to endow you with a more expert ignorance. . . .
> For the rest, even were I silent, it is amply clear to you how
> little these trivialities contribute to morality or purity of life,
> which is the most important consideration of all. From this
> obviously follows my final point, namely that this unseemly
> battle of words tends neither to the general good nor to the

honor and profit of our country, which is generally considered the supreme purpose of all sciences. (Tillyard, p. 71.)

And note in this same attack on the scholastic philosophy, his concept of useful learning:

But let not your mind rest content to be bounded and cabined by the limits which encompass the earth, but let it wander beyond the confines of the world, and at the last attain the summit of all human wisdom and learn to know itself, and therewith those holy minds and intelligences whose company it must hereafter join. (*Ibid.*, p. 72.)

We are reminded of Plato here in the reminiscence of the Delphic 'Know thyself' which Socrates took as his maxim,[1] and again when the test of learning is made its use, not in a narrowly 'pragmatic' sense, but for the humane happiness by which every supposed good is to be measured. By this test, many kinds of knowledge are found wanting, and Milton condemns them always in the same terms:

These studies promote neither delight nor instruction, nor indeed do they serve any useful purpose whatsoever. (Tillyard, p. 68.)

The word by which Milton expresses his contempt of false learning is 'sophistry.' It is Plato's word, and we know from the *Reason of Church-Government* (3. 202), and from the *Apology for Smectymnuus* (3. 293-4), that Milton associated it with Plato. In the Third *Prolusion,* where he first spoke his dislike of scholastic philosophy, Milton was already identifying waste and abuse of study with false teaching, deriding the 'warty controversies of the sophists' (C.E. 12. 159),[2] and characterizing the 'moulders of sophis-

---

[1] Compare Milton's definition of 'a true knower of himself' as one 'in whom contemplation and practice, wit, prudence, fortitude, and eloquence' meet. (*Church-Gov.* 3. 186.)

[2] In this passage and the one on the next page, the Columbia translation shows the point more clearly than Mrs. Tillyard's.

tries' in the manner of Plato as 'inclined by some innate tendency to quarrels and dissension, prating fellows moreover, and such as detest and ever turn away from sound and wholesome wisdom' (Tillyard, p. 70). Thenceforth Milton constantly drew an ever clearer line between knowledge and the 'Lernaean swamp of sophisms, contrived for shipwreck and destruction' (C.E. 12. 277); until in the *Reason of Church-Government* he finally declares that the 'thorny lectures of monkish and miserable sophistry . . . [have] stopped and hindered all true and generous philosophy from entering' (3. 273).

This opposition of 'sound and wholesome wisdom' to its deceptive semblance is Plato's own; and for Milton, his opponents in theology and politics adequately fill the role assigned in the Dialogues to the tribe of Sophists. Pretenders to learning, ignorant of all correct doctrine, eager for pay, careless of the true end of instruction, they represent the very antithesis of the scholars whose company Milton wished to join, and their fancied erudition the opposite of the studies that foster life. But however sternly Milton and Plato reject 'the foreign, the superfluous, the useless,' in learning, and however harsh their constant censure of the 'dangerous deceiver' with his 'sly shuffle of counterfeit principles,' they both retain the conviction that pursuit of knowledge is the activity for which man was intended. And although difficult, the pursuit is the avenue to happiness.

The concept Milton held of the knowledge worth this toil and of its use in rendering man happy appears throughout his works. Oliver Morley Ainsworth has collected a number of relevant excerpts in his edition of the Tractate *Of Education*, and Ida Langdon's study of *Milton's Theory of Poetry and Fine Art* bears upon the problem. But for our present purpose, a single passage from the *Reason of Church-Government* will suffice:

How happy were it for this frail and, as it may be truly called, mortal life of man, since all earthly things which have the name of good and convenient in our daily use, are withal so cumbersome and full of trouble, if knowledge yet, which is the best and lightsomest possession of the mind, were, as the common saying is, no burden; . . . for not to speak of that knowledge that rests in the contemplation of natural causes and dimensions, which must needs be a lower wisdom as the object is low, certain it is that he who hath obtained in more than the scantest measure to know anything distinctly of God, and of his true worship, and what is infallibly good and happy in the state of man's life, what in itself evil and miserable, though vulgarly not so esteemed, he that hath obtained to know this, the only high valuable wisdom indeed, . . . cannot but sustain a sorer burden of mind and more pressing than any supportable toil or weight which the body can labor under; how and in what manner he shall dispose and employ those sums of knowledge and illumination which God hath sent him into this world to trade with. (3. 229.)

The constituents of 'the only high valuable wisdom' which Milton here names are precisely those set for the advanced training of the guardian class in the *Laws*. Knowledge of 'natural causes and dimensions' is, as Plato thought it, a 'lower wisdom.' The higher is not easy to win, and when won, becomes a responsibility to its possessor. Like Plato, Milton is fully aware of the debt imposed on the few who can win the knowledge that constitutes the happiness of all men. Always with the consciousness of 'gifts of God's imparting' must go the 'fear lest they be reckoned many rather than few' (3. 282); always the philosopher must conceive of himself 'as a member incorporate into that truth' (3. 284) which he has won. The Platonic view that philosophers must take upon themselves the burdens of society, not resting in contemplation, but returning to instruct and guide the benighted dwellers in the Cave; this view, which has seemed to many an inconsistency in Plato, is precisely Milton's understanding of the function of knowledge.

If Milton or Plato had supposed that the highest truth resides in any knowledge but that of good and evil, we might find them less unwilling to accept contemplation divorced from practice as the great source of happiness. Plato is often thought to have done this very thing, but hardly by so careful a student as Milton. The entire design of the *Republic* is to show the proper relation of reason, will, and appetite, not merely in the individual, but in the organically unified State. The *Laws,* again, is deeply concerned with the practical life of the body politic. And the glorified Socrates of the Dialogues consistently engages in the social work of stinging his fellow-citizens to learn and practice the good life. Plato nowhere praises a reclusive contemplation at the cost of social benefit. He could not and still retain his belief that ethical studies are the knowledge in which human happiness is rooted. And similarly Milton, accepting ethics as the architectonic science, must regard true knowledge and practice as one; or to use his own terms, he cannot regard 'discipline' as anything but 'the execution and applying of doctrine home' (3. 6).

Thus far we have found a marked similarity between Milton's view of knowledge and the belief of Plato that philosophy is the highest good for man. Their rejection of sophistical learning is merely the negative aspect of a high faith in true knowledge rightly used. Milton moves from an early enthusiasm for studies to a conviction, more pronounced in his later writings, that the noblest study, unlike inferior kinds, bears within itself what is needed for individual and social well-being. But he has a test for 'sound doctrine' that Plato could not have, the explicit revelation of truth by God. And emboldened by possessing an indubitable standard, he can judge and condemn realms and modes of thought with a finality that we shall not find in the Dialogues. Yet his judgments, although determined by another principle, resemble those of Plato, since he had assimilated Platonic teaching to the essential doctrines of Christianity.

Both *Paradise Lost* and *Paradise Regained,* where Biblical influence is dominant, retain the Platonic views of knowledge that permeate Milton's less theological writings. In the first description of Adam we are reminded of the end which Plato set as man's chief good:

> For contemplation hee and valour form'd.

There is throughout the poem high praise of philosophy, by implication and often by negation, as when Milton describes the fallen angels in debate:

> Of good and evil much they argu'd then,
> Of happiness and final misery,
> Passion and Apathy, and glory and shame,
> Vain wisdom all, and false Philosophy. (2. 562-5.)

What Milton says of empty and erroneous thought must not be taken as his judgment of a serious inquiry into ethical truth. We are to remember in every encounter with the fallen angels that they are Sophists all. Milton does his best to warn us, using terms much like the Platonic account of false rhetoric; Satan's words bear

> Semblance of worth, not substance. (1. 529.)

And Belial owes at least one sentence in the description of him to Plato's character of the Sophists:

> A fairer person lost not Heav'n; he seem'd
> For dignity compos'd and high exploit:
> But all was false and hollow; though his Tongue
> Dropt Manna, and *could make the worse appear*
> *The better reason,* to perplex and dash
> Maturest Counsels: for his thoughts were low. (2. 110-5.)

He is the archetype of false rhetorician, but all the Satanic troop are members of one family.

In *Phaedrus*, we remember, Socrates distinguished the subjects wherein deception is possible as the disputable class of things, such topics as justice, goodness, love, or, briefly, the realm of ethics. Now merely because Milton, like Plato, recognizes this as the field for Sophists, we are not to suppose he thinks it their property. Before he himself could write *Paradise Lost* Milton had to probe the very questions discussed by his sophistical fallen angels,

> Providence, Foreknowledge, Will, and Fate,
> Fixt Fate, free will, foreknowledge absolute. (2. 559-60.)

Only, whereas they 'found no end, in wand'ring mazes lost,' he did reach solutions, having presumably avoided their mazes of self-deception. Those who have rejected the source of all Truth could hardly discuss such questions without error; he, having started from the right point in his inquiry, could complete it satisfactorily.

Commentators generally find it hard to allow the counsel Raphael gives to Adam on the quest for knowledge:

> Be lowly wise:
> Think only what concerns thee and thy being. (8. 173-4.)

But this again is a corollary to the Platonic principle of Milton's ethics: the secondary is always dangerous when not subordinated to the primary. We have the clue to his meaning in the Argument prefixed to Book 8:

Adam inquires concerning celestial Motions, is doubtfully answer'd, and exhorted to search rather things more worthy of knowledge.

Knowledge is still good, though its various branches are more and less worthy of pursuit. We must reckon with the time and circumstances of Raphael's admonition if we are not to misinterpret. We know from *Areopagitica* that Milton sympathized with Galileo, who dared think 'in astronomy otherwise than the Franciscan and Dominican licensers thought.' And Raphael cannot be a mere licenser, setting bounds to a scientific curiosity on the part of Adam. Look back at the answer Uriel made to Satan, who disguised his intent in visiting the new world as

> Unspeakable desire to see, and know
> All these [God's] wondrous works, but
> chiefly Man.

The 'Regent of the Sun' and 'sharpest-sighted Spirit of all in Heav'n' applauded the desire

> which tends to know
> The works of God, thereby to glorify
> The great Work-Master;

and thought that it

> leads to no excess
> That reaches blame, but rather merits praise.
> (3. 662-97.)

Milton himself in earlier years had praised a like interest:

The more deeply we delve into the wondrous wisdom, the marvelous skill, and the astounding variety of its [the universe's] creation (which we cannot do without the aid of Learning), the greater grows the wonder and awe we feel for its Creator and the louder the praises we offer Him, which we believe and are fully persuaded that He delights to accept. (Tillyard, p. 108.)

Recall the argument in the *Laws* on this same question. Plato has the Athenian make astronomy a study of the guardian-class, and then affirm:

It is currently said that it is wrong—indeed, positively blasphemous—to prosecute inquiry or busy ourselves with the quest for explanation where the Supreme God and the universe as a whole are concerned—though the very opposite should seem to be our right course. (7. 821.)

The reason for this view is given more fully in *Timaeus:*

Sight, then, as I hold, is the cause of our chiefest blessing, inasmuch as no word of our present discourse of the universe could have been uttered, had we never seen stars, sun, nor sky. As it is, the vision of day and night, months and circling years, equinoctials and solstices, has created number, given us the notion of time, and moved us to search out universal nature; hence we have derived philosophy, than which no greater boon has been, nor ever shall be, bestowed by heaven on mortality. This, then, I say is the chief blessing of eyesight. . . . God invented it and bestowed it on us that we might perceive the orbits of understanding in the heavens and apply them to the revolutions of our own thought that are akin to them, the perturbed to the imperturbable, might learn to know them and compute them rightly and truly, and so correct the aberrations of the circles in ourselves by imitating the never-erring circles of the god. (47.)

Noting that Plato praises astronomical study for giving knowledge of the gods, and thereby improving human nature, we can better understand why Uriel praises in the dissembling Satan, and Raphael discourages in Adam, a curiosity about the same sphere of learning. The 'divine Historian' has already merited thanks from Adam for having

> allay'd
> The thirst I had of knowledge, and voutsaf't
> This friendly conversation to relate
> Things else by me unsearchable, now heard
> With wonder, but delight, and, as is due,
> With glory attributed to the high
> Creator. (8. 7-13.)

But Adam's fond inquiry is next,

> How Nature wise and frugal could commit
> Such disproportions,

making all Heaven revolve about 'the sedentary Earth.'

And still Raphael reaffirms the notions Plato held about this study:

> To ask or search I blame thee not, for Heav'n
> Is as the Book of God before thee set,
> Wherein to read his wond'rous Works, and learn
> His Seasons, Hours, or Days, or Months, or Years.
>
> (8. 66-9.)

So far astronomy is useful; but the remainder of Adam's inquiry Raphael disparages:

> God to remove his ways from human sense,
> Plac'd Heav'n from Earth so far, that earthly sight,
> If it presume, might err in things too high,
> And no advantage gain. . . .
>
> Heav'n is for thee too high
> To know what passes there; be lowly wise:
> Think only what concerns thee and thy being. (8. 119-74.)

Milton, we see, is still insisting upon the hierarchy of learnings, and still measuring study against study by the human advantage to be gained. The precept, 'Be lowly wise,' reminds us of the Platonic letter he had written years before to Diodati. Seeking by the guidance of *Phaedrus* for the Idea of the Beautiful, he was then meditating flight into the high realms of poetry; but having found the wings of his Pegasus as yet too tender, he made his maxim *'Humile sapiamus.'* In knowledge as in art the first steps must be humbly made, and Adam may not yet be ready for the astronomical rung in the ladder of science. Blake and Wordsworth and Whitman would certainly have agreed with Raphael that Adam can do better at this stage than become a learned astronomer. Moreover, this speech of Raphael sends us back to an earlier passage in *Paradise Lost:*

> So little knows
> Any, but God alone, to value right

> The good before him, but perverts best things
> To worst abuse, or to thir meanest use. (4. 201-4.)

Adam still good and happy can accept the doctrine as Plato and Milton accepted it; a useless knowledge is no knowledge at all. He can even apologize for his ill-timed question:

> But apt the Mind or Fancy is to rove
> Uncheckt, and of her roving is no end;
> Till warn'd, or by experience taught, she learn
> That not to know at large of things remote
> From use, obscure and subtle, but to know
> That which before us lies in daily life,
> Is the prime Wisdom; what is more is fume,
> Or emptiness, or fond impertinence,
> And renders us in things that most concern
> Unpractis'd, unprepar'd, and still to seek. (8. 188-97.)

As in the Tractate *Of Education* and throughout Milton's writings, so here, in Paradise on the point of being lost, the proper study of mankind is ethics. Raphael will gladly help Adam inquire 'into the ways of God with Man.' This is of course the inquiry of *Paradise Lost* itself, and Milton points the analogy by using the very words with which he had concluded his first invocation of the Muse. The Eighth Book with its discourses on knowledge good and and evil prepares us to see the real error in the later choice of the forbidden fruit; for God has not deprived Adam of the right to know. When Adam named the animals as they passed, he understood

> Thir Nature, with such knowledge God endu'd
> My sudden apprehension. (8. 353-4.)

This understanding of the lower orders of creation was useful to him who was to be their master. In every way Milton assures us before the fall that the fruit offered no knowledge at all, and could produce nothing either necessary or useful to man's happiness. The point would seem too obvious for statement did not readers again and again miss the intention of Milton's account. Some would even have us think the fall a necessary prelude to the highest happiness; but they are deceived, like our original parents, by the argument that good can be known only by experience of evil.

Undeceived, Milton does his best to warn the reader. Nor may we accept the interpretation of those who put the burden of this, to them strange, view of knowledge on its Biblical source. Milton chose the plot of his epic poem with great care, after much deliberation; and the theory of knowledge involved in the fall is central to the story. Moreover, Milton deliberately elaborates this part of the fable, and, since he could not find material for the elaboration in his primary source, uses the philosophy he thought closest to Scriptural teaching in order to emphasize the wrong view of knowledge which causes man and woman to lose their happiness. From Plato he takes the principle by which Raphael warns Adam:

> Knowledge is as food, and needs no less
> Her Temperance over Appetite, to know
> In measure what the mind may well contain,
> Oppresses else with Surfet, and soon turns
> Wisdom to Folly, as Nourishment to Wind. (7. 126-30.)

If Plato made knowledge itself the measure of temperance, Milton converts this highest principle of the Platonic ethics into one yet higher. For Plato the end of man is to know and enjoy knowledge for ever; for Milton it is to glorify God and for ever enjoy Him. Thus Adam in his state of innocence thanks the archangel:

> Well hast thou taught the way that might direct
> Our knowledge, and the scale of Nature set
> From centre to circumference, whereon
> In contemplation of created things
> By steps we may ascend to God. (5. 508-12.)

There is a knowledge by which man ascends to comprehension of his Maker. So, too, thought Plato; but in the Christian Maker there is a purpose for man that Plato did not comprehend. Love is the final standard of conduct in the Christian view, love of God with its necessary and inseparable companion, love of neighbor. As the highest virtues in the Platonic scale, wisdom and its companion, justice, are displaced by the Christian virtues, so knowledge, the food of reason, must yield to faith, the food of love, as the most desirable of goods. Eve and Adam after her break faith in disobeying God's commands, reverse the scale of values, thinking to raise knowledge above trust, and thus fall from love and wisdom, faith and knowledge, all at once. As Plato had made the science of good and evil and its attendant virtue of wisdom the keystone of all happiness, upon which the right use of every other good depends, so Milton places the trustful acceptance of God's will and its attendant virtue of love. Remove the keystone, according to either scheme, and the entire structure of human well-being topples to the ground. Exactly as Plato had held that a courage and temperance not founded in knowledge were not courage and temperance at all, for Milton a knowledge not rooted in faith is only the false semblance of knowledge.

Elsewhere, in his treatise *De Doctrina Christiana,* Milton explicitly states the relations between faith and knowledge, love and wisdom, which are the essential teaching of *Paradise Lost:*

Christian doctrine is comprehended under two divisions: *Faith, or the knowledge of God; and Love, or the worship of God.* . . . Obedience and love are always the best guides to knowledge. . . . It must be observed, that Faith in this division does not mean the habit of believing, but the things to be habitually believed. (14. 23-5.)

Man was made in the image of God, and had the whole law of nature . . . implanted and innate in him, . . . which is sufficient of itself to teach whatever is agreeable to right reason, that is to say, whatever is intrinsically good. (15. 115-7.)

This death [from sin] consists, first, in the loss, or at least in the obscuration to a great extent, of that right reason which enabled man to discern the chief good, and in which consisted as it were the life of the understanding. . . . It consists, secondly, in that deprivation of righteousness and liberty to do good, and in that slavish subjection to sin and the devil, which constitutes, as it were, the death of the will. (15. 207.)

Evil works downward in Plato's view: destroy the virtue of reason, and the virtues of will and appetite will die. Similarly Milton, going a step beyond Plato, keeps to the same way of thought: if the highest good, faith, is destroyed, reason cannot know, the will choose, nor appetite enjoy, in right and happy fashion. What further explanation do we need to perceive the consistency of Milton's view of knowledge? Test by this standard the sophistical words of the tempter, who—be it remembered—did *not* taste the apple:

> O Sacred, Wise, and Wisdom-giving Plant,
> Mother of Science, Now I feel thy Power
> Within me clear, not only to discern
> Things in thir Causes, but to trace the ways
> Of highest agents, deem'd however wise. (9. 679-83.)

And test again the arguments by which he would persuade Eve to be

> Deterr'd not from achieving what might lead
> To happier life, knowledge of Good and Evil;
> Of good, how just? of evil, if what is evil
> Be real, why not known, since easier shunn'd?
> God therefore cannot hurt ye, and be just;
> Not just, not God. (9. 696-701.)

The lie of a Sophist must always approach the truth if it is to be convincing; and Milton here allows to Satan the half-truth which is the contradiction of the whole. Too many readers confuse Satan's lie with the truth Milton speaks in *Areopagitica:*

Good and evil we know in the field of this world grow up together almost inseparably; and the knowledge of good is so involved and interwoven with the knowledge of evil, and in so many cunning resemblances hardly to be discerned, that those confused seeds which were imposed on Psyche as an incessant labor to cull out and sort asunder were not more intermixed. It was from out the rind of one apple tasted that the knowledge of good and evil as two twins cleaving together leapt forth into the world. And perhaps this is that doom which Adam fell into of knowing good and evil, that is to say of knowing good by evil. (4. 310-11.)

Like lesser men, Milton may stretch a point in the effort to persuade; but still there is distinction enough between his argument and Satan's to warrant our belief that Milton did not allow the tempter to speak the truth. First of all, the 'knowing good by evil' is in Milton's phrase a 'doom which Adam fell into,' in Satan's a guide to 'happier life.' Secondly, the situation has been completely reversed: Adam, instructed by God, possessed the useful knowledge; we, ignorant since the fall, must seek what Adam lost, and must therefore seek it upon new conditions. We have no advantage in the necessity imposed upon us of learning good through evil, and Milton does not call it an advantage, but simply a necessity. And finally, if Milton admits that from 'one apple tasted . . . the knowledge of good and evil . . . leapt forth into the world,' he is not among those who rejoice in the twin-birth of such knowledge as fallen Adam can win.

At any rate, throughout *Areopagitica* Milton speaks from the very premise that Satan suppresses in his argument: not the knowledge itself, but the use of it is all-important. The syllogism might have ended differently, had Satan said with Milton:

The knowledge cannot defile . . . if the will and conscience be not defiled. (4. 308.)

Conversely, if the will and conscience be defiled, the knowledge cannot 'lead to happier life'; for if Milton compares knowledge to 'meats and viands, some of good, some of evil substance,' and thinks God 'left arbitrary the dieting and repasting of our minds,' trusting man 'with the gift of reason to be his own chooser,' he yet agrees with Raphael, not Satan, that knowledge 'needs no less her temperance over appetite.' The sum of Milton's argument in *Paradise Lost* is as it is in *Aeropagitica*:

How great a virtue is temperance, how much of moment through the whole life of man. (4. 309.)

Chosen for a wrong purpose, on false grounds, and at the cost of a higher good, the apple produced no knowledge save that of

Good lost and Evil got,
Bad Fruit of Knowledge, if this be to know. (9. 1072-3.)

What else do we expect? As C. S. Lewis points out, the apple is merely an apple. It is not a condensed encyclopedia. Its sole virtue was as a pledge; and the pledge broken, Adam and Eve win no knowledge at all in the sense of understanding, but only the experience of misery. The fatal *double entendre* catches many a reader off-guard.

But to know evil by doing and suffering it is not true knowledge, as repentant Adam is only too eager to admit. In his speech to Michael, the problem begins to be resolved:

Greatly instructed I shall hence depart,
Greatly in peace of thought, and have my fill
Of knowledge, what this Vessel can contain;
Beyond which was my folly to aspire.

Henceforth I learn, that to obey is best,
And love with fear the only God. (12. 557-62.)

And the final resolution comes in Michael's reply, the final
words of superhuman understanding that end the converse
of mankind with Heaven:

This having learnt, thou hast attain'd the sum
Of wisdom; hope no higher, though all the Stars
Thou knew'st by name, and all th' Ethereal Powers,
All secrets of the deep, all Nature's works,
Or works of God in Heav'n, Air, Earth, or Sea; . . .
only add
Deeds to thy knowledge answerable, add Faith,
Add Virtue, Patience, Temperance, add Love,
By name to come call'd Charity, the soul
Of all the rest: then wilt thou not be loath
To leave this Paradise, but shalt possess
A Paradise within thee, happier far. (12. 575-87.)

They miss the point who think that Milton sets Adam's
degenerate state above the state of innocence. Michael
compares not the paradise within, which Adam has already
lost, with that which he yet may find, but the external Eden
with the inner; for the final consequence of the fall is this
disjoining of inner and outer state. Happiness may yet be
won in this life, but no longer with the circumstantial ease
of a state where knowledge of good was not twin-born with
knowledge of evil. Look to the end of Michael's words, and
see how much 'happier far' the inner state is now to be,
when all mankind shall live,

though sad
With cause for evils past, yet much more cheer'd
With meditation on the happy end. (12. 603-5.)

The happy end, moreover, is now to be attained only by
a labor 'above heroic, though in secret done.' We must turn

to *Paradise Regained* for the view Milton ultimately took of the relations between happiness and knowledge.

Lest we lose our way in the subtle controversies of *Paradise Regained,* let us repeat the 'sum of wisdom' from Michael's final instruction of Adam. Though man knew all the secrets of physics and astronomy, he could know no more than this, that obedience and love are the source of every other human good. Love is 'the soul of all the rest'; without it, knowledge, like pleasure, wealth, and far-famed power, crumbles to worthlessness. There are no separate goods for man. Happiness can grow in one soil only; in every other the seeds of every lesser joy become sterile.

What then becomes of the Platonic view that knowledge is the chief good? In *Paradise Regained* we shall find it, as in *Paradise Lost* but more clearly, taking the place of fame as the 'last infirmity of noble mind.' Jesus, the Everyman of the poem, recalls that in his youth

> all my mind was set
> Serious to learn and know, and thence to do
> What might be publick good; myself I thought
> Born to that end, born to promote all truth,
> All righteous things: therefore above my years,
> The Law of God I read, and found it sweet,
> Made it my whole delight, and in it grew
> To such perfection, that ere yet my age
> Had measur'd twice six years, at our great Feast
> I went into the Temple, there to hear
> The Teachers of our Law, and to propose
> What might improve my knowledge or their own. (1. 202-13.)

The arch-sophist is clever to reserve knowledge for the final temptation. But even before we hear Jesus and Satan in debate, we are aware that knowledge is not the main end, and therefore not the main source of strength, for this man. Unlike Adam, where knowledge fails him he can say:

> Perhaps I need not know;
> For what concerns my knowledge God reveals. (1. 292-3.)

From the first, he declares that God provides

> In pious Hearts, an inward Oracle
> To all truth requisite for men to know. (1. 463-4.)

Satan hazards a reference to the first fall, assuring Jesus that the food he offers

> no knowledge works, at least of evil. (2. 371.)

And we are convinced that Milton did not think the knowledge won by Adam worth its price. This time Satan will not offer so obviously poor a bargain. But first he flatters the intellectual pride of his opponent, as the Sophist always flatters the instinct on which he plans to work:

> I see thou know'st what is of use to know,
> What best to say canst say, to do canst do;
> Thy actions to thy words accord, thy words
> To thy large heart give utterance due, thy heart
> Contains of good, wise, just the perfect shape. (3. 7-11.)

Satan is preparing to use a seeming Platonism as his final bait. And yet even here Milton makes apparent the sophistry of the tempter. If Jesus already possesses 'of good, wise, just, the perfect shape,' what further need he know?

Perhaps Milton overemphasizes the sophistical nature of the antagonist, and yet the Satan of *Paradise Regained* fools as many as the Satan of *Paradise Lost,* for the 'Rhetoric that sleeks the tongue' of Jesus' tempter is persuasive. Satan begins his argument with words so close to Milton's own in the early prolusions and poems, that we listen amazed:

> Be famous then
> By wisdom; as thy Empire must extend,
> So let extend thy mind o'er all the world,
> In knowledge, all things in it comprehend. (4. 221-4.)

The second step adds the lie that turns the whole to false-hood:

> All knowledge is not couch't in Moses' Law,
> The Pentateuch or what the Prophets wrote,
> The Gentiles also know, and write, and teach
> To admiration, led by Nature's Light;
> And with the Gentiles much thou must converse,
> Ruling them by persuasion as thou mean'st,
> Without thir learning how wilt thou with them,
> Or they with thee hold conversation meet? (4. 225-32.)

The offer of universal knowledge and with it the power of universal persuasion is ever the mark of the Sophist in Plato; and if we need another sign, Satan gives it in his next maxim:

> Error by his own arms is best evinc't. (4. 235.)

Socrates did not think so in spite of Anytus, Polus, and the rest, and Jesus is not more likely to admit that anything but truth can conquer falsehood.

So much for the grandiose pretenses of the temptation. But what of the knowledge itself that Jesus rejects? Let us take, as sample of it, the best:

> To sage Philosophy next lend thine ear,
> From Heaven descended to the low-rooft house
> Of Socrates, see there his Tenement,
> Whom well inspir'd the Oracle pronounc'd
> Wisest of men; from whose mouth issu'd forth
> Mellifluous streams that water'd all the schools
> Of Academics old and new, with those
> Surnam'd Peripatetics, and the Sect
> Epicurean, and the Stoic severe;
> These here revolve, or, as thou lik'st, at home,
> Till time mature thee to a Kingdom's weight;
> These rules will render thee a King complete
> Within thyself, much more with Empire join'd. (4. 272-84.)

This is the very rule over oneself, the very kingship of

philosophy, that Plato called the highest good, and Socrates is made first teacher of this wisdom. Milton evidently has added the scene to the traditional account of the temptation in order that *Paradise Regained* may represent the whole procedure by which man may win happiness.

But what exactly is the temptation that Jesus here overcomes? We must look to the answer he makes:

> Think not but that I know these things; or think
> I know them not, not therefore am I short
> Of knowing what I ought: he who receives
> Light from above, from the fountain of light,
> No other doctrine needs, though granted true. (4. 286-90.)

The Neoplatonic image of light that Milton uses had been fused with Manichean thought and popularized in the Christian schools by Augustine and his followers; and we may well turn to Augustine for help with the doctrine here advanced; for Augustine, next to the Bible itself, guided Milton in theology; and Augustine had dealt with this problem alien to Biblical thought. In the *Confessions,* he says of the time he spent in pagan studies: 'I had my back to the light, and my face to the things enlightened' (4. 16). And asking what it profited him to have known these things, he answers: 'Nothing.' Yet Augustine continued to make use of pagan thought long after his conversion, never attempting to rid his mind of all but Biblical and patristic lore. Apparently he distinguished not so much between a Christian and a pagan learning, as between a Christian and a non-Christian use of learning. His maxim was *'nisi crederitis, non intelligeritis'*: only he who has faith can understand the truth in any thought, and he who has faith needs no other measure of truth.

The notion was not peculiar to Milton in the seventeenth century, however odd it may now seem. Ralph Cudworth, another Christian Platonist, explains it at some length:

Knowledge indeed is a thing far more excellent than riches, outward pleasures, worldly dignities, or anything else in the world besides holiness, and the conformity of our wills to the will of God; but yet our happiness consisteth not in it, but in a certain Divine temper and constitution of soul which is far above it.

But it is a piece of corruption, that runneth through human nature, that we naturally prize truth more than goodness, knowledge more than holiness. We think it a gallant thing to be fluttering up to heaven with our wings of knowledge and speculation; whereas, the highest mystery of a divine life here, and of perfect happiness hereafter, consisteth in nothing but mere obedience to the Divine will. Happiness is that inward sweet delight that will arise from the harmonious agreement between our wills and God's will. There is nothing contrary to God in the whole world, nothing that fights against him but self-will. . . . It was by reason of this self-will that Adam fell in Paradise; that those glorious angels, those morning stars, kept not their first station, but dropped down from Heaven like falling stars, and sunk into the condition of bitterness, anxiety and wretchedness, in which now they are. They all entangled themselves with the length of their own wings, they would needs will more and otherwise than God would will in them; and going about to make their wills wider, and to enlarge them into greater amplitude, the more they struggled they found themselves the faster pinioned, and crowded up into narrowness and servility; insomuch that now they are not able to use any wings at all, but inheriting the serpent's curse, can only creep with their bellies upon the earth.[3]

If the doctrine is hard for those less faithful than Augustine, Cudworth, and Milton to accept, we are not therefore to think them inconsistent in holding it. Milton, far more than most admirers of knowledge, sought it actively, but kept firmly in view what gave knowledge its value.

---

[3] Quoted by Grierson in *Cross Currents in English Literature of the Seventeenth Century*, pp. 227-8, from *The Works of Ralph Cudworth* (1829), Vol. 4, Sermon 1.

So with the stern judgment here. Satan has promised Jesus all knowledge, and then offered the partial and imperfect philosophy of Greece separated from the one source of truth without which all knowledge is vain. If Jesus decries the 'sage philosophy' of Satan's offer as

> false, or little else but dreams,
> Conjectures, fancies, built on nothing firm, (4. 291-2.)

the falsity comes not in the doctrines themselves, but in their lack of firm foundation.

> Who therefore seeks in these
> True wisdom, finds her not, or by delusion
> Far worse, her false resemblance only meets,
> An empty cloud. (4. 318-21.)

And still we must ask, What of him who seeks, like Milton himself, to supplement the higher truth of revelation from these lesser sources? Jesus answers:

> Who reads
> Incessantly, and to his reading brings not
> A spirit and judgment equal or superior,
> (And what he brings, what needs he elsewhere seek)
> Uncertain and unsettl'd still remains,
> Deep verst in books and shallow in himself. (4. 322-7.)

A part of this answer we find elsewhere in Milton, as when he counsels his young acquaintance, Richard Jones:

There is also a well-equipped library; but unless it enables the students to improve their minds by the best instruction, it would deserve the name of 'book repository' rather than of 'library.' (Tillyard, p. 35.)

And again, when he mocks an opponent thus:

A learned man?—you that even unto your old age seem rather to have turned over phrase-books and lexicons and glossaries than to have perused good authors with judgment or profit; so that you prate of naught but manuscripts and various readings and dislocated passages and scribal errors, but show that you have drunk never the least drop of more substantial learning. (7. 67.)

Milton was always aware that the scholar must bring to his book 'a spirit and judgment equal or superior,' lest he fall into the vices of the pedant or, worse still, the Sophist; but would he also grant, what readers of *Paradise Regained* are loath to admit, that what the scholar brings he need not seek in his book? Perhaps Milton is here letting Jesus pay Satan with his own coin; perhaps he plays with the words 'spirit' and 'judgment,' and means that these alone the scholar cannot find in his book, while *food* for the spirit and judgment he may find; or perhaps neither the context nor the words will help us to escape from the apparent meaning that ancient wisdom can be useful only to him who does not need it. For Milton does a strange thing at the end of *Paradise Regained;* he shows that Jesus has won every good that Satan offered him, a banquet, power un-limited, and universal fame, every good indeed that man-kind strives for, won them all and with them happiness for all mankind, by refusing each of them separately. Only knowledge is not explicitly named in the reward which his faith earns.

We have reckoned thus far without the superhuman na-ture of Jesus. If we take the poem as theological rather than ethical, the difficulty disappears. The perfect man, the Man Divine, after all, needs no external help, but com-municates directly with the source of truth. But, unfortu-nately, the ethical meaning then disappears along with the difficulty. Milton intended *Paradise Regained* to show Jesus *winning* over Satan a victory that any man in any time could win. We are not to assume the victory from the beginning as predicated on a mystery, but rather to learn from it that for every man faith is the root and strength of all knowledge, and that for the man who perfects himself in faith all knowledge will rise directly from his communion with God. Once again hear Milton on our understanding and its object:

The very essence of Truth is plainness and brightness; the darkness and crookedness is our own. The wisdom of God created understanding, fit and proportionable to Truth the object and end of it, as the eye to the thing visible. If our understanding have a film of ignorance over it, or be blear with gazing on other false glitterings, what is that to Truth? (3. 33.)

Learning is, after all, a mere tool for purging the sight; the vision of Truth is finally the only knowledge; and since faith alone can attain that vision for understanding, the chief good of mankind lies, not, as Plato thought, in intellectual concepts however lofty, but in union of the whole spirit with its Maker. When reason beholds the Good, Plato would say, every part of the soul has its appropriate satisfaction, and enjoys the happiness of justice. Milton, converting the principle, would rather maintain that, in order to satisfy reason as well as every lesser faculty, the soul must live in God, and thence receive the only knowledge that can lead to happiness.

CHAPTER VI

The Theory of Ideas

WHEN Milton refused to knowledge the place of chief good, he did not discard, but amended, Platonic teaching. A part of that teaching, generally held the most distinctive part, is the much-disputed theory of Ideas. The theory is doubtless basic to all Plato's thought, but is presented in so many ways and attended by so many difficulties that scholars have been far from certain about its meaning. Popularly, the Platonic Idea is conceived of as an eternal archetype, remote from this world, yet productive of the whole corresponding class of earthly things, and related to them as a pattern or stamp to its reproduction or impress. The popular conception has grounds in the Dialogues, but there are grounds for doubting it too. Plato himself suggests the major arguments against Ideas of this kind, in some dialogues makes little or no use of the doctrine, and nowhere explicitly asserts that there is an Ideal pattern for every class of things. In general, when the doctrine of archetypes is presented as indisputable, the Idea is an ethical concept, Justice, Beauty, Goodness, or the like. When questions of an Ideal bed or animal are raised, the matter is left in doubt. For these reasons the theory has seemed to many scholars an attempt to support the universal stability of ethical truth rather than to effect a dichotomy of life into two distinct worlds.

Our aim is to find the meaning and use of the doctrine for Milton, and less to unravel the intricate questions it involves. Milton clearly had pondered them, arguing in his collegiate exercises and later whether 'form' could exist apart from matter; knew from Aristotle down the objections to the theory; and came to his own conclusions about Plato's meaning. According to Herbert Agar the doctrine of Ideas 'does not seem to have influenced Milton's thought, though he makes use of it four times as a convenient method of expression' (p. 18). But the four times Agar lists are not the only times Milton employs the doctrine, and are not merely convenient modes of expression.

Examine first some occurrences of the word 'idea' in Milton's writing (I mark with a star those that Agar has not considered):

* 1 For who can worthily gaze upon and contemplate the *Ideas* of things human or divine, unless he possesses a mind trained and ennobled by Art and Learning, without which he can know practically nothing of them? (Tillyard, p. 107.)

2 De *Idea* Platonica quemadmodum Aristoteles intellexit.

* 3 Neither tresses of gold nor rosy cheek beguiles me thus; but, under a new *form* [*nuova idea*], strange beauty charms my heart. (Sonnet 4, tr. by Smart, p. 150.)

4 Ceres never sought her daughter Proserpine (as the legend tells) with greater ardor than I do this *Idea* of Beauty [τοῦ καλοῦ ἰδέαν], like some image of loveliness; ever pursuing it, by day and by night, in every shape and form ('for many forms there are of things divine') and following close in its footprints as it leads. (Tillyard, p. 14.)

* 5 That which is thus moral, besides what we fetch from those unwritten laws and *ideas* which nature hath ingraven in us, the Gospel . . . lectures to us. (3. 197.)

* 6 If therefore the question were in oratory whether a vehement vein throwing out indignation or scorn upon an object that merits it were among the aptest *Ideas* of speech to be al-

lowed, it were my work, and that an easy one, to make it clear both by the rules of best rhetoricians and the famousest examples of the Greek and Roman orations. (3. 312.)

7 I . . . will forthwith set down in writing, as you request me, that voluntary *idea,* which hath long in silence presented itself to me, of a better education. (Ainsworth, p. 52.)

8 Thence to behold this new created World . . . Answering his great *Idea.* (*P.L.* 7. 554-7.)

* 9 For the foreknowledge of God is nothing but the wisdom of God, under another name, or that *idea* of everything [*illa rerum omnium idea*], which he had in his mind, to use the language of men, before he decreed anything. (14. 65.)

*10 For it is neither impious nor absurd to say, that the *idea* [*ideam*] of certain things or events might be suggested to God from some extraneous source; since inasmuch as God had determined from all eternity, that man should so far be a free agent, that it remained with himself to decide whether he would stand or fall, the *idea* [*idea*] of that evil event, or of the fall of man, was suggested to God from an extraneous source. (14. 79.)

*11 Genus does not properly communicate essence to species (since in itself it is in truth nothing outside the species) but merely signifies their essence, for the notion of what is essential and common to all species is called *genus,* and by the Greeks often *idea* [*idea*], but not separated from things, as they think the Platonic ideas are, which are clouds, according to Aristotle (*Metaphysics* 1. 7; 12. 5), but what in thought and reason is one and the same thing common to many species in each of which in fact and nature it appears singly, as Plato says in the *Meno.* The Stoics, however, as Plutarch reports (*De placitis philosophorum* 1. 10), said that ideas were our notions. (11. 239.)

Without arguing about his correctness, we may learn from these passages how Milton interpreted the doctrine. And first, since he uses the term 'idea' four times out of eleven as distinctively Platonic, in all likelihood he consistently associated it with Plato's usage. Secondly, he dismisses the objection of Aristotle that the Platonic 'Idea,' if a self-sustaining entity apart from all its manifestations, is a mere cloud, and cites Plato's own words to show how it may be distinct from, and yet in particular things. Thirdly, he duly assigns to the Stoics, and not to Plato, the view that ideas owe their existence to human thought. Fourthly, he is sure that some ideas, apparently of an ethical nature, are so far independent of our thinking them as to be innately impressed upon our minds. Fifthly, he believes that an essential common nature manifests itself variously in varied objects, in and through which it must be sought. Finally, and most important for him as a poet, he conceives of the Idea as a pattern in the creative mind, divine or human, according to which a world or treatise or series of events may be shaped. Rightly or wrongly, this is Milton's view of the Platonic doctrine of Ideas, and as such he often uses it in his writing.

But we can hardly limit our discussion to Milton's use of the word 'idea,' since Plato himself had many expressions for the concept. After the centuries of intervening discussion, Milton naturally employs various ways of stating the doctrine. Of his alternate terms, 'form' and 'essence' are most important, *forma* having been the regular Latin translation for Plato's ἰδέα or εἶδος, and *essentia* for οὐσία, the ideal being of an object. Insofar as Aristotle refined the concepts of form and essence without refuting Plato's view, Milton tries to keep his use of the terms consistent with both Plato and Aristotle. Thus in his *Logic* he offers the definition:

Form is the cause through which a thing is what it is. This definition joins those of Plato and Aristotle. For Plato defines form as the cause through which, Aristotle as that which is. (II. 59.)

And again:

That the form can also be the end Aristotle testifies. . . . And Plato in the *Philebus* lays down the essence or form of the thing as the end of generation. (11. 67.)

In using these concepts of an inner form or essence correlative with a function or effect, Milton consistently keeps to his definitions; and hence if he takes his definitions to be Platonic, we may regard the passages written in accordance with them as illustrations of the influence the Platonic theory of Ideas had on his thought.

In this sense, the pamphlets on the Church, on kingship, and on matrimony, are products of Plato's doctrine, for in all of them Milton is concerned with true or ideal form and proper function. See, for example, how he speaks of marriage:

The internal *Form* and soul of this relation is conjugal love arising from a mutual fitness to the final causes of wedlock, help and society in religious, civil, and domestic conversation, which includes as an inferior end the fulfilling of natural desire and specifical increase: these are the final causes both moving the efficient and perfecting the *form*. (4. 101.)

And further:

This gives marriage all her due, all her benefits, all her being, all her distinct and proper being. (4. 106.)

So again in *Colasterion* he asks concerning marriage:

How can a thing subsist when the true essence thereof is dissolved? (4. 262.)

And in *De Doctrina Christiana* he answers:

But if the essential form be dissolved, it follows that the marriage itself is virtually dissolved. (15. 157.)

His treatment of political and religious institutions is the same; only when the thing corresponds to its ideal or proper form and function may it be said to exist at all. A king is not a man born to the office, but he who fulfils the office of a king:

Where the Parliament sits, there inseparably sits the King, there the laws, there our oaths, and whatsoever can be civil in religion. They who fought for the Parliament, in the truest sense fought for all these; who fought for the King divided from his Parliament, fought for the shadow of a King against all these, and for things that were not, as if they were established. (5. 243.)

This use of Plato's figure of a shadow to express unreality in comparison with true existence shows Milton to be speaking the language of the Ideas. Again in castigating prelates, he keeps his 'spiritual eye' on the 'inward beauty and splendor' (3. 191) of the Church, and chides:

Believe it, wondrous doctors, all corporeal resemblances of inward holiness and beauty are now past; he that will clothe the Gospel now intimates plainly that the Gospel is naked, uncomely, that I may not say reproachful. (3. 246-7.)

Of those who changed from 'the simplicity and plainness of Christianity' to idolatrous ritual he says:

The beauty of inward sanctity was not within their prospect. (3. 25.)

These are but samples of a habit of thought constant with Milton, the Platonic habit of regarding, not the outer appearance, but the inner meaning, the 'Idea' of the thing. The reader may turn to almost any page of Milton's prose and later poems and find further examples of the pervasive influence of Plato's doctrine of the Idea as the true being, essence, or form of the varied phenomena of nature and human life.

The theory is far less pervasive in his earlier works than the myths through which Plato taught it. What does he

take the Platonic Idea to be in his verses on the subject?
A poetic fiction prosaically misinterpreted by Aristotle. The
festival of the gods, which in *Phaedrus* is the grand occasion for sight of the Ideas, is far more prominent in the
early poems of Milton than the Ideas themselves. There are
references to it in his obituary verses for the Bishop of
Winchester (41-50), in his Fifth *Elegy* (13-24), *On the
Nativity* (147-8), and elsewhere; the clearest is in lines
33-6 of the *Vacation Exercise:*

> Such where the deep transported mind may soar
> Above the wheeling poles, and at Heav'n's door
> Look in, and see each blissful Deity
> How he before the thunderous throne doth lie.

Similarly, the myth which makes a beloved person an
embodiment of the Ideas serves Milton as a poetic device
in various early poems, perhaps most strikingly in the lines
on *A Fair Infant* (53-6):

> Or wert thou Mercy that sweet smiling Youth?
> Or that crown'd Matron, sage white-robed Truth?
> Or any other of that heav'nly brood
> Let down in cloudy throne to do the world some good?

But the fancy for the myth connected with the doctrine
of Ideas turns later to a sober understanding of their ethical
importance. When Milton came to believe in an essential
form of marriage, of kingliness, of religious worship, that
determines and gives validity to their occurrence in mar-
riages, kingships, and religious institutions, he came to believe in the essential and universal reality of ethical concepts. On this point Agar writes:

Ethical philosophers, such as Plato and Milton, must by
nature look upon the moral world either as a realm of permanent
truths which are unaffected by the accidents of mortality, or
else as just another realm of flux, a repetition of the disorder
and impermanence which dominate the physical world, where

nothing is but what is not. These two classes of thinkers will be divided by their opinions, not only of the good and the bad, but of the beautiful and the ugly, the true and the false, and all that concerns philosophy. Agreement on this primary question is at least the basis for a bond of sympathy; and it will not be necessary to prove that here the views of Milton and Plato coincide. The statement that change is *not* the order of the moral world would seem true in the highest degree to both of these thinkers, and in the highest degree important. This statement, however, would be concurred in by a number of philosophers, and would not in itself prove any such affinity as I have been claiming. (Agar, p. 2.)

But we have every reason to believe that Plato's statements of the view were of singular importance to Milton, and of an importance far beyond any other philosopher's. The belief that the moral world is 'a realm of permanent truths' has not been generally shared by those on whom Plato had no influence; for it takes some defense, and Plato's theory of Ideas is among the most solid defenses as yet offered. If Milton was convinced that justice, beauty, and the like are unalterable realities, he made the Platonic 'Ideas' the basis of his conviction. Occasionally his choice of words proves this, as for example in *Comus,* when two Christian virtues and a virtue next of kin to Plato's 'temperance' are hypostasized:

> O welcome pure-ey'd Faith, white-handed Hope, . . .
> And thou unblemish't form of Chastity,
> I see ye visibly. (212-5.)

True, Milton may here be using the Platonic 'form' as a convenient poetic expression; and so again in *Paradise Regained:*

> Thy heart
> Contains of good, wise, just, the perfect shape. (3. 10-11.)

But in prose we may expect him to use only the sober expression that fits his thought; and yet we find the same imagery in the *Reason of Church-Government:*

Should not he rather now by his own prescribed discipline have cast his line and level upon the soul of man, which is his rational temple, and by the divine square and compass thereof form and regenerate in us the lovely shapes of virtues and graces? (3. 191.)

This passage from the *Reason of Church-Government* is explained by another, already quoted to illustrate Milton's use of the word 'idea.' There he speaks of 'those unwritten laws and ideas which nature hath ingraven in us,' here of the 'lovely shapes of virtues'; and in both places he has in mind the Platonic Ideas, and the Platonic theory that we are born with a knowledge of them. As a Christian, Milton rejects Plato's explanation that we won this knowledge in a previous existence, that is, he rejects the doctrines of metempsychosis and recollection; but he finds a convenient substitute in St. Augustine's theory that God himself imparts knowledge of the eternal Ideas to the human mind. (See, for example, *De Civitate Dei* 11. 10, F-G, I; and *De Diversis Quaestionibus* 46, entitled *De Ideis.*) Indeed, it is partly because Augustine accepted this theory and adapted it to Christianity that Milton found himself spiritually at home in the Platonic system of ethics with its absolutely valid Ideas. By making the Wisdom, Justice, Truth, and Beauty of Plato's scheme identical with the essence of God, and calling all other universals thoughts in the mind of God, Augustine gave the Platonic theory a new support. Formerly an objector could argue that the universal Ideas, since they are not of this world, could *be* nowhere; now, if a Christian, he would have to admit the divine mind as a place not only possible, but appropriate to their existence.

In the universality Milton attributes to moral concepts

we find the main influence of the theory of Ideas on him. But where else could we look? Even the young Milton ridiculed the prosaic habit of seeking eternal archetypes such as an Ideal Man, or seeking them in space and time. The very nature of the Idea is that it is to be sought only with the mind's eye, and only in realms explored by an inner vision. The doctrines of ethical thought are its proper habitat; an eternally valid Justice, Wisdom, Truth, are the proper examples to look for; and these we find so abundant in Milton's poetry and prose that we can scarcely present an exhaustive collection of them. Let a few illustrations suffice.

Take, then, the Platonic affirmation in Milton's Seventh *Prolusion:*

> While the other virtues are easily put to flight, Justice from her throne compels homage, for without her even the most unjust States would soon fall into decay. (Tillyard, p. 114.)

And compare his immediate source in the *Republic* 1. 352:

> We have already shown that the just are clearly wiser and better and abler than the unjust, and that the unjust are incapable of common action; nay more, that to speak as we did of men who are evil acting at any time vigorously together is not strictly true, for if they had been perfectly evil, they would have laid hands upon one another; but it is evident that there must have been some remnant of justice in them, which enabled them to combine; if there had not been they would have injured one another as well as their victims; they were but half-villains in their enterprises; for had they been whole villains, and utterly unjust, they would have been utterly incapable of action.

That Justice maintains even unjust organizations only a Platonist could believe, only one who held with Plato that Justice absolute is a reality from which the more and less just derive their phenomenal existence. To this Justice absolute, God affirms Adam's punishment is due:

Die hee or Justice must. (3. 210.)

This is the Justice which Milton calls in the *Doctrine and Discipline of Divorce* 'the queen of virtues' (3. 473), and in the *Tenure of Kings* 'the only true sovran and supreme majesty upon earth' (5. 41). For Milton's English poems Bradshaw lists in his *Concordance* some 121 occurrences of the word 'just' and its derivatives. Milton shows his readers how to interpret the word, in a long discussion in *Eikonoclastes:*

> For me, though neither asked nor in a nation that gives such rewards to wisdom, I shall pronounce my sentence somewhat different from Zorobabel, and shall defend that either Truth and Justice are all one, for Truth is but Justice in our knowledge, and Justice is but Truth in our practice; . . . or else, if there be any odds, that Justice, though not stronger than Truth, yet by her office is to put forth and exhibit more strength in the affairs of mankind. . . . Though wicked kings and tyrants counterfeit her sword, as some did that buckler fabled to fall from heaven into the Capitol, yet she communicates her power to none but such as like herself are just, or at least will do justice. For it were extreme partiality and injustice, the flat denial and overthrow of herself, to put her own authentic sword into the hand of an unjust and wicked man. (5. 292-3.)

In this passage, we see two Platonic Ideas, Justice and Truth, contending for supremacy; and while awarding higher rank to one, Milton affirms, as Plato affirmed, that there is a unity behind even the Ideal entities, a single Idea of which these are aspects much as phenomena in turn are aspects of them. In any case, Truth like Justice is for Milton absolute and independent of particular truths, giving to them, not gaining from them, real existence. Thus in his Fifth *Prolusion:*

> For invincible Truth has within herself strength enough and to spare for her own defence, and has no need of any other help;

and though she may seem to us at times to be hard-pressed and beaten to the ground, yet she maintains herself ever inviolate and uninjured by the claws of Error. (Tillyard, pp. 84-5.)

This is the Truth for serving which Abdiel is praised:

> Servant of God, well done; well hast thou
>   fought
> The better fight, who single hast maintain'd
> Against revolted multitudes the Cause
> Of Truth, in word mightier than they in Arms;
> And for the testimony of Truth hast borne
> Universal reproach, far worse to bear
> Than violence. (6. 29-35.)

This is the Truth which the Jesus of *Paradise Regained* thought himself 'born to promote' (1. 205), and for which Socrates lived and died,

> For truth's sake suffering death unjust. (3. 98.)

Bearing in mind the 'perfect shape' of 'good, wise, just,' in *Paradise Regained* 2. 11, we shall recognize in two passages from the *Reason of Church-Government* and *Areopagitica* the visible stamp of Plato's theory of Ideas. In the first Milton says:

For Truth, I know not how, hath this unhappiness fatal to her, ere she can come to the trial and inspection of the understanding; being to pass through many little wards and limits of the several affections and desires, she cannot shift it, but must put on such colors and attire as those pathetic handmaids of the soul please to lead her in to their queen. . . . And contrary, when any falsehood comes that way, if they like the errand she brings, they are so artful to counterfeit the *very shape and visage* of Truth, that the understanding . . . sentences for the most part one for the other at the first blush. (3. 249.)

And again:

Truth indeed came once into the world with her divine Master, and was a *perfect shape* most glorious to look on; but when he ascended and his Apostles after him were laid asleep, then straight arose a wicked race of deceivers, who . . . hewed *her lovely form* into a thousand pieces and scattered them to the four winds. . . . We have not yet found them all, Lords and Commons, nor ever shall do, till her Master's second coming; he shall bring together every joint and member, and shall mold them into *an immortal feature of loveliness and perfection.* (4. 337-8.)

The 'shape' of Truth in both these passages is not merely a personification, but an instance of the Platonic ἰδέα, the form visible to the inner eye. A sentence in the *Defensio Secunda* suggests that Milton, like Augustine and the Bible, identified at least this one of the absolute essences with God:

God himself is truth; and the more closely any one adheres to truth, in teaching it to mankind, the more nearly must he resemble God, the more acceptable must he be to him. (8. 65.)

But those absolute forms and eternal shapes of moral concepts are so numerous throughout Milton's writings that we cannot undertake to list all their appearances. Let it suffice to prove his acceptance of the doctrine, that he added to the ideal essences which appear in the Dialogues his own Idea of Discipline. So thoroughly Platonic is his conception of it that the passage in *The Reason of Church-Government* might be an excerpt from any of the longer speeches of Socrates:

There is not that thing in the world of more grave and urgent importance, throughout the whole life of man, than is discipline. What need I instance? He that hath read with judgment of nations and commonwealths, of cities and camps, of peace and war, sea and land, will readily agree that the flourishing and decaying of all civil societies, all the moments and turnings of human occasions, are moved to and fro as upon the axle of discipline. So that whatsoever power or sway in mortal things weaker men have attributed to fortune, I durst with more confidence (the honor of Divine Providence ever saved) ascribe either to the vigor or the slackness of discipline. Nor is there any sociable perfection in this life, civil or sacred, that can be above discipline; but she is that which with her musical cords preserves and holds all the parts thereof together. . . . And certainly discipline is not only the removal of disorder, but *if any visible shape can be given to divine things, the very visible shape and image of virtue;* whereby she is not only seen in the regular gestures and motions of her heavenly paces as she walks, but also makes the harmony of her voice audible to mortal ears. (3. 184-5.)

We cannot expect in poetry, or even in prose not of a strictly scientific nature, the same rigorous distinction that philosophers who derive their idealism from Plato maintain between a world of flux and a world of permanent realities. The poet, like Plato himself in his more poetic dialogues, will use the Ideal World to show what in the scope of human affairs moves toward, or accords with, the transcendent reality; and so, too, the writer on practical affairs, like Plato himself in his teaching of ethics and politics, will use the supraterrestrial realm to measure and to explain the phenomena of seeming reality. Thus Milton generally uses the Ideas, and yet occasionally he takes the Platonic duality more emphatically as a cleavage between two worlds. We see it in *Paradise Lost* when he describes that

> Portal, . . . inimitable on Earth
> By Model, or by shading Pencil drawn. (3. 508-9.)

Again, Raphael makes the distinction in teaching Adam:

> What surmounts the reach
> Of human sense, I shall delineate so,
> By lik'ning spiritual to corporeal forms,
> As may express them best, though what if Earth
> Be but the shadow of Heav'n, and things therein

> Each to other like, more than on earth is
>   thought? (5. 571-6.)

As Raphael takes earth to be the shadowy counterpart of heaven, so Michael suggests how man may eventually rise

> From shadowy Types to Truth, from Flesh to
>   Spirit. (12. 303.)

But in general, the 'very visible shape and image of virtue' is the main contribution of the Platonic world of true being to Milton's thought—and not only where a phrase reveals his source, but throughout the moral substructure of his writings. Everywhere in Milton's work, more vaguely in earlier years, more distinctly later, belief in the clearly defined and unalterable nature of moral truth is of the essence of his poetry and prose. Thus the eternal decrees of Justice in *Paradise Lost* illustrate the absolute validity of *principles* as opposed to the fluctuations of occurrence, and so, too, in *Paradise Regained* the triumph of Good through Truth, Wisdom, and Justice. This teaching is the contribution of the 'divine volumes' that Milton celebrated in the *Apology for Smectymnuus*.

In yet another way, quite foreign to Plato, the theory of Ideas entered the substance of Milton's work. Through the pagan Neoplatonists the Ideas become Intelligences as well as intelligibles, and thence by easy steps the angels of Neoplatonic Christians. We know that Milton was familiar with this conversion of the Platonic Ideas, for in his copy of Dante's *Convivio* he marked as worthy of note the section dealing with the transformation:

There were others, like Plato, a most eminent man, who assumed not only that there are as many Intelligences as there are movements of the heaven, but also as many as there are species of things, just as there is one species for all men, and another for all gold, and another for all riches, and so on; and they would have it that as the Intelligences of the heavens are producers of these movements, each one of its own, so these other Intelligences are producers of everything else, and exemplars each one of its own species; and Plato called them 'ideas,' which is equivalent to calling them universal forms and natures. (2. 5, trans. by W. W. Jackson.)

Even before Milton undertook to write of the angelic hierarchies, we see the Platonic Idea in his heavenly creatures in such a passage as this from his Third *Prolusion:*

[Let your mind] learn to know itself, and therewith those holy minds and intelligences whose company it must hereafter join. (Tillyard, p. 72.)

The advice is like that of the Dialogues, except that 'those holy minds and intelligences' have replaced the Ideas. Once this is clear, we may see in the angels of *Paradise Lost* and the fallen angels of both *Paradise Lost* and *Paradise Regained* the Platonic essences transformed into the 'Intelligences of the Heavens.' To trace that metamorphosis is beyond our scope, but we may suggest one of the links in the chain that starts from the Ideas of Beauty, Goodness, Justice, and the like, and ends with the robust figures of Raphael and Michael. The change is in process in the Neoplatonic *Liber de Causis,* a work popular in Dante's time, where the imperishable universals of Plato are in process of becoming heavenly spirits.

But that is a separate tale of philosophical, religious, and literary continuity, while ours is of an immediate transfer and assimilation of a philosophical doctrine by a poet. Or shall we say of a poetical doctrine? In the verses *De Idea Platonica,* Milton had called Plato a poet for creating this very doctrine. And it seems unreasonable to suppose Milton untouched by a theory that had permeated European thought in one way or another from Plato's time to his own, or to think that he could have admired the volumes of Plato and ignored their most distinctive teaching. The Idea did not mean to him precisely what it means to Santayana or Whitehead; but Milton could hardly have entertained the concepts of universal reality or arrived at the vision of human circumstances *sub specie aeternitatis* without which *Paradise Lost, Paradise Regained,* and *Samson* are inconceivable, had he not won from his reading in Plato the view of stability behind apparent flux that is named the theory of Ideas.

CHAPTER VII

The Doctrine of Love

WHEN Milton substituted faith and love for knowledge and wisdom as the keystone of happiness, we may say that he proceeded from a Platonic to a supra-Platonic ethics. But Milton himself forces us to modify the statement. The very passage in the *Apology for Smectymnuus* where he speaks of his debt to Plato asserts that what he primarily learned from the Dialogues was a theory of love. Let us once more attend to his now familiar words:

Thus, from the laureate fraternity of poets, riper years and the ceaseless round of study and reading led me . . . to the divine volumes of Plato; . . . where, if I should tell you what I learned of chastity and love, I mean that which is truly so, whose charming cup is only virtue, which she bears in her hand to those who are worthy (the rest are cheated with a thick intoxicating potion, which a certain sorceress, the abuser of love's name, carries about), and how the first and chiefest office of love begins and ends in the soul, producing those happy twins of her divine generation, knowledge and virtue, with such abstracted sublimities as these; it might be worth your listening, readers, as I may one day hope to have ye in a still time, when there shall be no chiding. (3. 305.)

Our first question must be, What was the doctrine of love that thus enchanted Milton? Having found that, and the use to which he put the doctrine, we shall have to see why, if knowledge is Love's own child, Milton deliberately replaced knowledge by love as the chief means to happiness.

Before resolving these questions, it is worth observing that, far beyond the common opinion of him, Milton was a poet of love in the tradition of the Renaissance, as genuinely as constant treatment of its themes could make him. The word 'love' in various forms and compounds occurs some one hundred and eighty times in his English poems alone, and the early Latin and Italian verse is predominantly concerned with *amor* and *amore*. Still, apart from some distinctively Ovidian elegies and *sylvae*, even in his earliest work Milton takes love to be something more than the natural affection between the sexes. Thus in the elegy for *A Fair Infant*, he speaks of 'heav'n-lov'd innocence,' certain that man is not only ruled, but loved, by God. The same sense of God's surpassing care for man reappears in the verses *Upon the Circumcision*, where the poet asks and answers himself on the mediation of Christ:

> O more exceeding love or law more just?
> Just law indeed, but more exceeding love!

But it is not primarily the love of God for man that pervades Milton's writing, though almost always this hovers about his use of the word, purifying and enriching his concept of what human love can be with the assurance that God himself loves and *is* Love. More often Milton is concerned with man's own love, frequently with that love which Michael at the end of *Paradise Lost* teaches Adam is the soul of all other virtues, love—

> By name to come call'd Charity.

The word 'charity' is used only two other times in Milton's English poems; usually 'love' does service for the Christian virtue, as in the lines *On Mrs. Thomason:*

> When Faith and Love which parted from thee never,
> Had ripen'd thy just soul to dwell with God. (1-2.)

And here in the love that 'ripens the just soul' we come very close to the doctrine that Milton professed to have learned from Plato. We must leave the distinction in his thought between Platonic and Christian love until we have first examined Plato's concept.

The two dialogues that deal most extensively with the nature of love, *Phaedrus* and the *Symposium,* were favorites in the Renaissance, especially among poets. Ficino, Pico della Mirandola, and Castiglione placed upon these two works an emphasis so extraordinary that 'Platonic love' speedily came to be the one thing Platonic of which, then as now, the generality heard. In Spenser's *Four Hymns* honoring love and beauty, we find the impress of these Platonizing Italians; and let us at once add, the impress is still recognizably Platonic. However distorted the teaching may have become in lesser minds and lesser hands, those who seriously accepted it did not drive it far from the mark that Plato intended.

The speakers of the *Symposium* in their eulogies of Eros advance varied theories, the more important parts of which are caught up, interwoven, and transformed in Socrates' encomium of love. From Phaedrus' discourse he takes the notion that the lover is moved to virtue, especially in the presence of his beloved. From Pausanias comes the distinction between the heavenly and earthly Aphrodite, the heavenly and earthly love. Eryximachus enlarges the realm of love to include the universe, explaining all sympathetic and antipathetic movements as the effects of love and hate, and further separating love into the true harmony of unlike elements and the false conjoining of destructive forces. From Aristophanes comes the myth of the two halves seeking, through love, reunion into an original whole, a myth destined to become famous in itself, and, through Aristotle's conversion of it, into a definition of the friend as 'another self.' Agathon finally adds the touch of lyric rapture, proclaiming love the best and fairest of things human and the cause of every other good, the original poet and source of all poetry, the delicate young god who brings order out of chaos and peace to the hearts of men.

If Plato intended these speeches to be entirely superseded by that of Socrates, he would hardly have composed them all with the excellence of structure and phrase that has won them a permanent hold on readers. And indeed Socrates' discourse surpasses rather than supersedes the previous accounts of love; for although, in his first insistent questioning of Agathon, he seems bent on destroying the premises of all the former speakers, his own further words belie that intention. In his supposed account of the lore of Diotima he uses the better part of the doctrines we have assigned to their first speakers. But Socrates combines and unifies these diverse reflections by defining love as the desire for eternal possession of the good, that is, as the yearning for happiness. Mythically born of Plenty and Poverty at the feast of Aphrodite, Love seeks the beauty which is good in order to beget the lover's likeness and thereby perpetuate him. In the realm of the common or earthly Aphrodite, this seeking and begetting mean marriage and children; in the realm of the Uranian Aphrodite, the lover ascends as on a ladder from physical beauty to spiritual, until he finally wins sight of Beauty absolute, and there brings to birth the realities of knowledge and virtue which constitute the happiness of man. Love thus defined is the generic longing for every good; its highest species is philosophy, the longing for wisdom or knowledge.

In *Phaedrus* again, love, inspired by visible beauty, gains for the soul the vision of transcendent Ideas; but here that vision is clearly a reward in the after-life. Through the images first of the winged soul, and then of the charioteer, reason, with his two horses of will and desire, Socrates teaches the need of continence if love is to bring happiness. The wing of the soul, fed by the sight of earthly beauty, droops at a lustful touch; the wild horse of desire, uncurbed by reason, and unimpeded by will, can delay by thousands of years the visionary bliss. Again, the highest kind of love is philosophy, the desire of knowledge, even if this must be gained through devotion to a particular person in whom the Idea, the true object of knowledge and therefore of love, manifests itself.

Now Milton specifically explains his understanding of Platonic love as (1) a distinction between love and lust; (2) a process that occurs in the soul; (3) a creator of knowledge and virtue; (4) a thing divine; and (5) an 'abstracted sublimity.' Starting with the last first, we note that the term 'abstracted sublimity' reflects the words of Diotima at the critical turn of her speech from earthly to heavenly love:

These are the lesser mysteries of love, into which even you, Socrates, may enter; to the greater and more hidden ones which are the crown of these, and to which, if you pursue them in a right spirit, they will lead, I know not whether you will be able to attain.[1]

Thus in *Comus*, the Lady refuses to teach her tormentor

> The sublime notion, and high mystery
> That must be utter'd to unfold the sage
> And serious doctrine of Virginity.

Her argument is,

> Thou hast nor Ear, nor Soul to apprehend.

But further,

> And thou art worthy that thou shouldst not know
> More happiness than this thy present lot. (784-9.)

Clearly Milton believes with Plato that the 'high mystery'

---

[1] *Symposium* 210 a. Compare the initiation into 'perfect mysteries' in *Phaedrus* 249 c.

of true love, which here, as in the *Apology for Smectymnuus,* is linked with the doctrine of chastity, brings happiness when understood. This belief sheds light on Milton's other uses of the Platonic teaching.

The first mysterious element in love, as Eryximachus and Socrates after him had explained, is its harmonizing power that pervades and sustains the universe. Milton has in mind this universal power when he speaks in *The Doctrine and Discipline of Divorce* about

the issues of love and hatred distinctly flowing through the whole mass of created things, and . . . [by God's doing ever bringing] the due likenesses and harmonies of his works together, except when, out of two contraries met to their own destruction, he moulds a third existence. (3. 418.)

Like the speakers in the *Symposium,* he is more concerned with those species of the generic love that directly affect human life. Human love arises, and here Milton cites Plato as an authority, from human need:

All ingenuous men will see that the dignity and blessing of marriage is placed rather in the mutual enjoyment of that which the wanting soul needfully seeks than of that which the plenteous body would joyfully give away. Hence it is that Plato in his festival discourse brings in Socrates relating what he feigned to have learned from the prophetess Diotima, how Love was the son of Penury, begot of Plenty in the garden of Jupiter. Which divinely sorts with that which in effect Moses tells us, that Love was the son of loneliness, begot in Paradise by that sociable and helpful aptitude which God implanted between man and woman toward each other. (3. 398.)

The need being in the soul, as a sense of imperfection long-ing to be perfected, it requires for its satisfaction not so much outward acts as inward assurance. With this convic-tion Milton writes to Diodati:

I would not have true friendship tried by the test of letters and good wishes, which may all be feigned; but its roots and the sources of its strength should go deep into the mind, and it should spring from a pure origin, so that, even were all tokens of mutual regard to cease, yet it should endure throughout life, untainted by suspicion or recrimination. For its nurture the written word is less essential than a lively recollection of virtues on both sides. Nor does it follow that, in default of your writing, there is nothing to supply the omission; your integrity writes to me in your stead, and indites true letters on the tablets of my heart; the purity of your life and your love of virtue write to me, your whole character too, far above the common, writes to me and commends you to me more and more. (Tillyard, p. 13.)

And some years later, lamenting Diodati's death, he declares of this harmony of friendship that it is desired and attained only by the noble spirit:

He [Love] does not aim at little souls and the ignoble hearts of the rabble, but, rolling his flaming eyes about, unwearied, he ever scatters his missiles on high through the spheres, and never aims his shot downward. Hence minds immortal and forms divine are inflamed with love. (MacKellar, p. 171.)

In the early Latin poems, and in his Italian sonnets with their Florentine Platonism, Milton had celebrated the perceptible beauty that moves to love and creates new gifts and powers in the lover. Like Phaedrus in the *Symposium,* he asserted that love and nobility of spirit are inseparable:

Truly is he destitute of all worth that is not moved to love by thy gentle spirit; which sweetly reveals itself—bounteous in pleasant looks, and the gifts that are the arrows and bow of Love—there, where blooms thy lofty might. When thou speakest in beauty, or singest in joy, . . . let him who is unworthy of thee guard well the entrance of his eyes and ears. Only grace from above may help him, ere amorous longing lingers in his heart. (Smart, p. 144.)

And again:

Love quickens on my swift tongue the new flower of a foreign speech, as I sing of thee, sweet and noble lady. . . . Love willed it; and I knew at the cost of others that Love never willed aught in vain. (*Ibid.*, pp. 146-7.)

Even while assuring Diodati that it was not physical beauty alone that enchanted him, he exalted the embodiment of the 'Idea' as the object of his love in the terms of Petrarchan Platonism:

Neither tresses of gold nor rosy cheek beguiles me thus; but, under a new form [*nuova idea*], strange beauty charms my heart. (*Ibid.*, p. 150.)

But with the letter he wrote to Diodati in 1637, his tone changes. Now it is no longer physical beauty that draws him, but the inward beauty of the noble soul which, Plato had taught, more truly reflects the perfect Idea of Beauty. The words suggest that Milton has learned Diotima's ultimate lesson: the true love of beauty is philosophy, love of wisdom.

Though I know not God's intent toward me in other respects, yet of this I am sure, that he has imbued me especially with a mighty passion for Beauty. Ceres never sought her daughter Proserpine (as the legend tells) with greater ardor than I do this Idea of Beauty, like some image of loveliness; ever pursuing it, by day and by night, in every shape and form ('for many forms there are of things divine') and following close in its footprints as it leads. And so, whensoever I find one who spurns the base opinions of common men, and dares to be, in thought and word and deed, that which the wisest minds throughout the ages have approved; whensoever, I say, I find such a man, to him I find myself impelled forthwith to cleave. (Tillyard, p. 14.)

In 'every shape and form,' says Milton, but clearly he reckons the impress of beauty on 'thought and word and deed' a higher token of the Beauty absolute than beauty of person. The outer beauty retains its fascination for him, but the inner excellence comes more and more to surpass it in his esteem.

When we turn now to the much misinterpreted tracts on divorce, we shall recognize that Milton is doing little more than apply his Platonic theory of love to the institution of marriage. Agar (p. 34, n. 2) rightly thinks *The Doctrine and Discipline of Divorce* among the most Platonic of Milton's writings. It is the immediate product of his thought on that love whose 'first and chiefest office . . . begins and ends in the soul.' Since it is 'the mind from whence must flow the acts of peace and love' (3. 93), there can never be true marriage save where 'the fit union of their souls be such as may even incorporate them to love and amity; but that can never be where no correspondence is of the mind' (3. 477-8). We need not labor the matter; throughout the tracts on divorce, Milton insists to the point of repetition that the essential union is of the soul, and that the true mate is 'another self, a second self, a very self itself' (4. 90). Only union of this kind enables man to rise to 'such a love as Christ loves his Church' (4. 192); all other union, under whatever name, is lust.

The theory of marriage and divorce that dominates these tracts, and asserts itself again in the treatise *De Doctrina Christiana,* depends upon the Platonic dichotomy of the world into two realms: the material, or that which affects the body, and the spiritual, or that which affects the soul. (See 15. 155-79.) Presumably Milton came in his later years to discard this separation, for in *De Doctrina Christiana* he affirms:

Man having been created after this manner, it is said, as a consequence, that 'man became a living soul'; whence it may be inferred (unless we had rather take the heathen writers for our teachers respecting the nature of the soul) that man is a living being, intrinsically and properly one and individual, not compound or separable, not, according to the common opinion, made up and framed of two distinct and different natures, as of soul and body, but that the whole man is soul, and the soul man, that is to say, a body, or substance individual, animated, sensitive, and rational. (15. 39-41.)

The heathen writers whose view is here rejected are clearly Plato and the Platonists.

Earlier, Milton had held the same view as Plato, that the body is not merely distinct from the soul, but a prison to it, and death consequently a release. The doctrine is reflected in *In obitum Praesulis Wintoniensis* 31-8, 41-50; the lines *On the Morning of Christ's Nativity* 13-4; *On Time* 4-8, 14-21; *Comus* 380-4, 419-80; and *On Mrs. Thomason* 3-4. Even in *Samson Agonistes* it is alluded to, if not affirmed:

> Thou art become (O worst imprisonment!)
> The Dungeon of thyself; thy Soul
> (Which Men enjoying sight oft without cause
>   complain)
> Imprison'd now indeed,
> In real darkness of the body dwells. (155-9.)[2]

Apparently even after he had discarded the belief that body and soul are separate entities, he could make dramatic use of it. At any rate, he never completely rejected the teaching of Plato on the relative worth of body and soul.

According to Plato, the body is inferior to the soul, at best its instrument, at worst its prison. And even when Milton adopts the Aristotelian concept of the soul as the form of the body (as in *Doct. Christ.* 15. 36-52), he retains the Platonic belief in the superiority of the soul. Thus of the mediatorial office of Christ's rule he writes:

Herein it is that the pre-eminent excellency of Christ's kingdom over all others, as well as the divine principles on which it is founded, are [sic] manifested; inasmuch as he governs, not the

---

[2] Cf. *Samson* 102 and 1572.

bodies of men alone, as the civil magistrate, but their minds and consciences. (15. 299.)

Whatever the strict explanation of the union of soul and body, the soul is always for Milton more important. And hence the persistence of his view that marriage is pre-eminently a joining of souls, and that love is pre-eminently the desire of the soul for happiness.

The psychology of Plato taught Milton that 'the Soul excels the body' (*Tetrach.* 4. 118), and that love of 'the souls of men . . . is the dearest love' (*Animad.* 3. 107). And the Platonic view of the soul had a further importance for Milton's theory of love. The tripartite division into reason, will, and desire, which is imaged in *Phaedrus* under the figure of the charioteer and his two horses, often recurs in the Dialogues, most significantly in the *Republic* 4. 441-3 and *Timaeus* 69-71. Agar (pp. 12-8) has shown beyond the need of further demonstration that Milton adopted this account of the soul. Reason, in his scheme as in that of Plato, is the noblest faculty and should therefore rule; the will, as the instrument of action, should carry out the decisions of reason; the appetites, as the lowest part of the soul and most closely bound to the body, should willingly obey the commands of the better part. And Milton accepted other doctrines connected with this analysis of the soul: the concept of tyranny as the rule of appetite, and of justice as the harmony of the three elements.

Another corollary of the Platonic psychology had an even more marked effect on Milton's thought. If the upstart reign of appetite is the root of error, it is at the same time its punishment. The worst of doing evil is that the soul becomes evil, goes to war with itself, and can never escape. Thus Milton berates an opponent in his *Pro Se Defensio* (9. 189):

But alas! wretch that you are! You have long been at dreadful variance with yourself! To you, nothing is more intolerable than to be, to dwell with yourself. . . . What raises such commotion within is, that within is a whip, and that Argus tormentor of yours . . . follows you ever . . . to disquiet you with the maddening gad-fly of your heinous crimes!

Vice is a disease that destroys the vicious, as God intimates in *Paradise Lost* when he says that, after Adam's fall, he will have to

> renew
> His lapsed powers, though forfeit and enthrall'd
> By sin to foul exorbitant desires. (3. 175-7.)

Thus Plato had explained evil and its punishment throughout the Dialogues. Evil is a disease, to be cured like a disease.

And hence the irony of the half-truth in Satan's first greeting of his new abode:

> Hail horrours, hail
> Infernal world, and thou profoundest Hell
> Receive thy new Possessor: One who brings
> A mind not to be chang'd by Place or Time.
> The mind is its own place, and in itself
> Can make a Heav'n of Hell, a Hell of Heav'n.
> What matter where, if I be still the same? (1. 250-6.)

The mind can doubtless make a 'Hell of Heav'n' as Satan did—but not, by the very nature of Hell *as* a state of soul, a 'Heav'n of Hell.' 'What matter where' indeed, so long as the Hell-making mind is 'still the same.' According to the eschatological myths of Plato, the soul gains for itself a habitation appropriate to it, and can no more create an external heaven for its inner hell than it can fail to turn every outer good into a further torment for itself. And therefore when Satan thinks to change his fortune by changing his place, he cannot leave behind

> The Hell within him, for within him Hell
> He brings, and round about him, nor from Hell
> One step no more than from himself can fly
> By change of place. (4. 20-3.)

He himself recognizes his self-inflicted doom:

> Me miserable! which way shall I fly
> Infinite wrauth, and infinite despair?
> Which way I fly is Hell; myself am Hell;
> And in the lowest deep a lower deep
> Still threat'ning to devour me opens wide,
> To which the Hell I suffer seems a Heav'n. (4. 73-8.)

He had thought to be free in the abyss, to 'reign secure' (1. 259-63), but security and freedom are not for the soul in which the tyranny of ambition and hatred has upset the rule of reason. As Milton puts it in his sonnet on those who think freedom can be theirs for the snatching,

> Licence they mean when they cry liberty,
> For who loves that, must first be wise and good.

Now he is wise in whom reason maintains harmony; he is doomed by his own folly in whom reason becomes the minister to base aims, and doomed to that ministry as well as by it. Only if he can shake off his self-imposed chains will he ever know release; and no external power can help except by inducing in him a change of desire; for a man is ultimately happy or wretched as he wants the right or wrong things. This is the essential teaching of Plato in ethics and psychology.

Our concern is more with the effect of that teaching on Milton's theory of love. The first effect is his distinction between love and lust. Since the mind is 'the worthiest part of man' (*Tetrach.* 4. 87), love manifests the rule of reason, whereas in lust reason and will surrender to appetite. *Comus* stresses the negative aspect of this theory: lust

'imbrutes' the soul, transforming her to the image of the
bestial appetites, while chastity turns the body itself 'to
the soul's essence' by 'driving far off each thing of sin and
guilt.' Were it not that Milton promised to speak of the
'abstracted sublimities' of love after he had written *Comus*,
we might think that poem the fulfilment of his promise, and
finding there only the negative doctrine of chastity, might
reasonably conclude that Milton's view of love was only
the lesser half of Plato's. But we know from the Cambridge
Manuscript that Milton included in three separate drafts for
a tragedy on the subject of *Paradise Lost* a figure that he
called 'Heavenly Love.' Here, then, was the poem in which
he intended to teach 'that love which is truly so'; and while
the epic poem that he finally wrote is doubtless far from
his original plan, *Paradise Lost* as it stands does perform
the teaching promised in the *Apology for Smectymnuus*.
'Heavenly Love,' the doctrine of the 'divine volumes' of
Plato, is a major theme in the explanation Milton gives of
the loss of happiness.

To the reader who is aware of Milton's former intention,
the first words on love in *Paradise Lost* begin to speak the
influence of Plato:

> Hail wedded Love, mysterious Law, true source
> Of human offspring, sole propriety,
> In Paradise of all things common else.
> By thee adulterous lust was driv'n from men
> Among the bestial herds to range, by thee
> Founded in Reason, Loyal, Just, and Pure. (4. 750-5.)

The 'mysterious Law' is the 'mystery of love' expounded
by Diotima; and love is distinguished from lust, as in
Plato's treatment, by being founded in reason. Milton repeats the distinction with emphasis when he declares of
the relation between Adam and Eve:

> Love unlibidinous reign'd. (5. 449.)

But only when we come to the dialogue in the Eighth Book between Adam and his angelic visitor, do we learn why Milton has been so emphatic in his first description of the love between Adam and Eve. As Adam relates how he asked God for a companion, we begin to hear the subtler themes of Platonic love. The myth of Diotima on the birth of Eros, Milton had said in *The Doctrine and Discipline of Divorce* (3. 398), 'divinely sorts with that which in effect Moses tells us, that Love was the son of Loneliness, begot in Paradise.' Here Adam reflects that 'divine agreement' between Diotima and Moses, explaining to God:

> Thou in thyself art perfet, and in thee
> Is no deficience found; not so is Man,
> But in degree, the cause of his desire
> By conversation with his like to help,
> Or solace his defects. (8. 415-9.)

To which the divine voice answered:

> What next I bring shall please thee, be assur'd,
> Thy likeness, thy fit help, thy other self,
> Thy wish, exactly to thy heart's desire. (8. 449-51.)

And now, with love, son of Plenty and Poverty, 'begot in Paradise,' the struggle to stand firm or fall begins. The beauty of Eve moves Adam as Plato had said beauty moves the lover:

> What seem'd fair in all the World, seem'd now
> Mean, or in her summ'd up, in her contain'd
> And in her looks, which from that time infus'd
> Sweetness into my heart, unfelt before,
> And into all things from her Air inspir'd
> The spirit of love and amorous delight. (8. 472-7.)

Raphael, like a wise Diotima or a wiser Socrates, attempts to instruct Adam in the 'higher mysteries,' not blaming his

attachment to Eve, but showing how he may make use of it
to gain perfect and lasting happiness:

> What higher in her society thou find'st
> Attractive, human, rational, love still;
> In loving thou dost well, in passion not,
> Wherein true Love consists not; love refines
> The thoughts, and heart enlarges, hath his seat
> In Reason, and is judicious, is the scale
> By which to heav'nly Love thou may'st ascend,
> Not sunk in carnal pleasure. (8. 586-93.)

The argument that Raphael uses is Plato's: the beauty of
Eve being external, is a thing inferior to the inner beauty
of Adam's wisdom; for Adam has admitted that

> All higher knowledge in her presence falls
> Degraded, Wisdom in discourse with her
> Loses discount'nanc't, and like folly shews. (8. 551-3.)

The Angel answers 'with contracted brow':

> Accuse not Nature, she hath done her part;
> Do thou but thine, and be not diffident
> Of Wisdom, she deserts thee not, if thou
> Dismiss not her, when most thou need'st her nigh,
> By attributing overmuch to things
> Less excellent, as thou thyself perceiv'st. (8. 561-6.)

Adam has begun to sever love from reason, to reverse the
scale of values by subordinating wisdom to physical beauty;
and Raphael sees at once where his error will lead if not
swiftly checked. Love can be the 'scale' to heaven only if it
does not forget that its proper object is the possession of
lasting good. Now lasting good in Christian thought is God
and God alone. And hence Adam's mistake in staying at the
first rung of the ladder instead of climbing to the highest
is, or is likely to become, the preference of Eve to God.
The warning of Raphael temporarily serves to recall Adam

to the proper nature of his love for Eve. Their love is not
the lustful reign of appetite, but

> Union of Mind, or in us both one Soul;
> Harmony to behold in wedded pair
> More grateful than harmonious sound to the ear. (8. 604-6.)

Further, Adam shows himself a good student by repeating
Raphael's lesson; he still keeps himself

> free [to]
> Approve the best, and follow what I approve.
> To love thou blam'st me not, for love thou
>   say'st
> Leads up to Heav'n, is both the way and guide. (8. 610-3.)

When Raphael answers the question whether the angels
love, we see another trace of the 'heavenly' love:

> Let it suffice thee that thou know'st
> Us happy, and without Love no happiness. (8. 620-1.)

No happiness without love of wisdom was Plato's creed;
substituting the omniscient God of Christianity for σοφία,
Milton's becomes: without love of God no happiness.

But the lower rungs of the ladder remain as in the
Platonic scheme. Personal love, according to Phaedrus in
the *Symposium,* inspires the lover to virtue. Thus Adam to
Eve:

> I from the influence of thy looks receive
> Access in every Virtue, in thy sight
> More wise, more watchful, stronger, if need were
> Of outward strength; while shame, thou looking on,
> Shame to be overcome or over-reacht
> Would utmost vigour raise, and rais'd unite. (9. 309-14.)

And so long as the affection is one that can 'lead up to
Heaven,' Adam may assure Eve that God made them for

> Love not the lowest end of human life.

> For not to irksom toil, but to delight
> He made us, and delight to Reason join'd. (9. 241-3.)

But when the delight of love is no longer 'to Reason join'd,' when Adam dignifies Eve beyond her proper worth, and ceases to desire what reason bids him desire, the scale is upset, and his love is no longer that which 'begins and ends in the soul, producing those happy twins of her divine generation, knowledge and virtue.' This is the catastrophe against which Raphael had given due warning, but at the critical moment Adam forgets the lesson.

The fall of Eve, as is often noted, closely follows the account in *Protagoras* of involuntary error. Misled by the serpent into thinking that she will be happier if she disobeys the command of God, she chooses an apparent good that is really an evil. Similarly Adam errs because he mistakes relative values, but his error is specifically that of irrational love. While Eve was a worthy object, the affection for her could be rational, ennobling, and therefore a step in the ascent to heavenly love. But as soon as love of her becomes a preference of her to God, that is to all good, Adam's love is no longer 'that which is truly so,' but the 'thick intoxicating potion' that 'abuses love's name.' Milton insists upon the distinction. Previously in their state of innocence,

> Love unlibidinous reign'd.

Now, with reason overthrown and the will powerless, the many-headed desires hold sway. Ironically, Milton recalls the allegory in *Phaedrus* of the winged soul:

> They swim in mirth, and fancy that they feel
> Divinity within them breeding wings
> Wherewith to scorn the earth. (9. 1009-11.)

But the wings that love might have bred in them are not, Milton would have us know, produced by sin:

> That false Fruit
> Far other operation first display'd,
> Carnal desire inflaming. (9. 1011-3.)

The rule of reason once broken, the reign of lust begins; and now, Milton insists,

> Love was not in thir looks, either to God
> Or to each other. (10. 113-4.)

Their loss of love for each other, a consequence of their loss of love for God, is the lowest point in the degradation of the pair. Happiness has been completely lost.

It remains for Adam to learn from a second angelic teacher how he may regain a measure of happiness by restoring his sense of values. The most important part of the lesson Adam makes clear:

> Henceforth I learn, that to obey is best,
> And love with fear the only God. (12. 561-2.)

Such loving and fearful obedience, by making Adam desire most what is most desirable, the merited possession of God's favor, will win him that favor, and therein he will find lasting happiness.

We now can see why Milton substituted love for knowledge as the mainspring of human joy, and how the theory of love which he learned from Plato led him to go beyond the Platonic scale of values. Since love is the moving impulse without which man rests content in his limited self, it becomes the source of every good, as it is the power which moves man to reach for the good that is not in him. And reason being the faculty that recognizes good, love is rational, beginning in the soul and desiring what will perfect it. Thus much Milton could learn from Diotima and Socrates: knowledge is the effect of love in action. But what precisely does love seek to possess and know? Plato had said that the object of love is an Idea, the perfect Beauty, the whole and complete Good. Christianity said that God alone is wholly good and perfectly beautiful; that is, Christianity identified God with the universals that Plato thought the ultimate object of knowledge. If God, then, becomes the proper goal of Christian philosophy, knowledge cannot be the highest aim of humanity, and this for the good reason that God is unknowable. Milton had declared in *De Doctrina Christiana* (14. 61): 'It follows, finally, that God must be styled by us *wonderful* and *incomprehensible.*' The Perfection by participating in which man becomes happy is then to be won, not by knowledge, but by love. And this love, this perpetual impulse to mount up to God, will of itself bring man to whatever knowledge is possible and valuable to him. In *Colasterion* (4. 264) Milton wrote:

For seeing love includes faith, what is there that can fulfil every commandment but only love?

Man may call his goal by the name of truth, but God alone is Truth (*Doct. Christ.* 14. 41). And therefore God alone is the right object of man's longing, and love alone the means of its fulfilment.

Much the same tale is retold in *Samson Agonistes*, except that the fall from right to wrong desire, being less fully intended than Adam's, is more easily repaired. Samson, like Adam, forgot at the critical moment where true good really lay; but unlike Adam he never argued himself into believing the false good true. He

> Whose strength, while virtue was her mate,
> Might have subdu'd the Earth, (173-4)

has fallen by 'impotence of mind, in body strong'; for, wisdom and virtue being one,

> What is strength without a double share
> Of wisdom? vast, unwieldy, burdensome,

> Proudly secure, yet liable to fall
> By weakest subtleties, not made to rule,
> But to subserve where wisdom bears command. (54-8.)

He has not sunk low enough to mistake his error, nor so low as those who are willing to come to terms with a fallen state,

> to love Bondage more than Liberty,
> Bondage with ease than strenuous liberty. (270-1.)

Samson is curable, and the cure, like the crime, grows out of a change of aim. The crime has brought its own penalty, the sense of God's favor lost, of evil merited. Nothing, Samson exclaims,

> Nothing of all these evils hath befall'n me
> But justly; I myself have brought them on,
> Sole Author I, sole cause. (374-6.)

And the outer punishment is only the expected reflex of the inner wrong:

> Servile mind
> Rewarded well with servile punishment!
> The base degree to which I now am fall'n,
> These rags, this grinding, is not yet so base
> As was my former servitude, ignoble,
> Unmanly, ignominous, infamous,
> True slavery, and that blindness worse than this,
> That saw not how degenerately I serv'd. (412-9.)

Therefore he will 'expiate, if possible' his crime—a crime which he explicitly calls a species of intemperance (558-62). The cure can be helped from outside; on that score Milton had long before accepted the opinion of Plato:

> He that will not let these [admonition and reproof] pass into him, though he be the greatest king, as Plato affirms, must . . . remain impure within. (*Church-Gov.* 3. 264.)

And even if admonition and reproof fail, according to

169

Plato, a soul not too far gone can be cleansed by the punishment which inevitably springs from crime. Samson is thus cleansed. Taught by his blindness and imprisonment where his true strength lay, steadied by all the trials of his visitants' counsel, reproaches, temptations, and taunts, victorious over his own pride and despair, when the last test comes, he knows what alone will bring him to peace. That is why the death he chooses is, even to his father, a triumph, not a catastrophe; it is Samson's conquest of himself as well as of the Philistines:

> And which is best and happiest yet, all this
> With God not parted from him, as was fear'd,
> But favouring and assisting to the end.
> Nothing is here for tears, nothing to wail
> Or knock the breast, no weakness, no contempt,
> Dispraise, or blame, nothing but well and fair,
> And what may quiet us in a death so noble. (1718-24.)

The purgation is accomplished; Samson has atoned, has made himself at one with the will of God, has regained in death the harmony that a foolish mistake in values had cost him in life. And God, having shown through his career how the lost good can be rewon,

> His servants he with new acquist
> Of true experience from this great event
> With peace and consolation hath dismist,
> And calm of mind all passion spent.

But there is a more direct road to happiness than the one Adam and Samson must take after they have lost their way. In *Paradise Regained* Jesus arrives at the desired end without a fall, by choosing from the first against every temptation the one sure source of joy. Milton has the angelic chorus sing before the trial begins:

> Victory and Triumph to the Son of God
> Now ent'ring his great duel, not of arms,
> But to vanquish by wisdom hellish wiles. (1. 173-5.)

As Agar says, Paradise is 'to be regained by a reassertion of the supremacy of reason over the passions' (p. 9). There is no talk of love as the one thing needful in *Paradise Regained;* there are no explicit statements to compare with the emphatic doctrine of heavenly love in *Paradise Lost.* Satan is no more the person to whom Christ would speak of that high mystery than Comus seemed a fit auditor to the Lady of the Mask. But, clearly enough, when Jesus reasserts the supremacy of reason, he is not asserting the purely Platonic notion that knowledge is the chief good. Far from it! He rejects knowledge as decisively as he had rejected pleasure, wealth, power, and fame, and always on the same ground: each of these is good, as Plato said and Milton repeated in *Samson Agonistes,* only to the good man, that is, only when added to that which can make it useful for human happiness. And for Milton that one irreplaceable source of all human good is loving trust in God. Jesus defeats his antagonist by wisdom, the virtue produced by knowledge, as Adam, Eve, and Samson were defeated through their foolish ignorance of true values. But the origins of that wisdom and that error are made clear at the beginning of *Paradise Regained* when Milton defines the themes of his two companion poems:

> I who erewhile the happy Garden sung,
> By one man's disobedience lost, now sing
> Recover'd Paradise to all mankind,
> By one man's firm obedience fully tried
> Through all temptation.

The Paradise that Adam lost and Jesus regained is the happiness of love, founded in trust, expressing itself in obedience to the moral law, and fulfilled in the perfect harmony of the soul within itself and with the divinely ordered universe which is its home.

A LIST OF REFERENCES TO PUBLICATIONS

EDITIONS AND TRANSLATIONS

Plato. Opera. Ed. by John Burnet. Oxford, 1896-1906.
    The Republic. Trans. by A. D. Lindsay. Everyman's Library, London, 1935.
    The Laws. Trans. by A. E. Taylor. London, 1934.
    On the Trial and Death of Socrates: *Euthyphro, Apology, Crito, Phaedo.* Trans. by Lane Cooper. Ithaca, New York, 1941.
    Phaedrus, Ion, Gorgias, and *Symposium,* with Passages from the *Republic* and *Laws.* Trans. by Lane Cooper. London, 1938.
    Timaeus and *Critias.* Trans. by A. E. Taylor. London, 1929.
    Dialogues. Trans. by Benjamin Jowett. New York, 1892.
    Glenn R. Morrow. Studies in the Platonic Epistles. Illinois Studies in Language and Literature 18, Nos. 3-4. Urbana, Illinois, 1935.
Milton. The Works of John Milton. Ed. by F. A. Patterson and others. Columbia University Press, New York, 1931-8.
    The Poems of John Milton. Ed. by Sir H. J. C. Grierson. London, 1925.
    The Latin Poems of John Milton. Ed. and trans. by Walter Mac Kellar. Cornell Studies in English, No. 15. New Haven, 1930.
    The Sonnets of Milton. Ed. and trans. by John S. Smart. Glasgow, 1921.
    Private Correspondence and Academic Exercises. Trans. by Phyllis B. Tillyard. Cambridge, 1932.
    Milton on Education. Ed. by Oliver Morley Ainsworth. Cornell Studies in English, No. 12. New Haven, 1928.

WORKS CITED

Agar, Herbert. Milton and Plato. Princeton Studies in English, No. 2. Princeton, 1928.
Ast, D. Friedrich. Lexicon Platonicum. Leipzig, 1835.
Aristotle. The Works of Aristotle. Ed. by W. D. Ross. Oxford, 1908-31.
Augustine. De Civitate Dei. Ed. by J. E. C. Welldon. London, 1924.
    The Confessions of Saint Augustine. Trans. by E. B. Pusey, ed. by Arthur Symons. London, 1898.
Baldwin, E. C. 'Milton and Plato's *Timaeus,*' PMLA. 35 (1920). 210-7.
    'A Note on *Il Penseroso,*' MLN. 33 (1918). 184-5.
Barker, Arthur. 'Milton's Schoolmasters,' MLR. 32 (1937). 517-36.

Campagnac, E. T. The Cambridge Platonists. Oxford, 1901.

Cassirer, Ernst. Die platonische Renaissance in England und die Schule von Cambridge. Leipzig, 1932.

Cicero. Three Books of Offices, etc. Trans. by C. R. Edmonds. London, 1916.

Dante. Convivio. Trans. by W. W. Jackson. Oxford, 1909.

Darbishire, Helen, ed. The Early Lives of Milton. London, 1932.

Diogenes Laertius. Lives of Eminent Philosophers. Ed. and trans. by R. D. Hicks. Loeb Classical Library, London, 1925.

Downham, George. Rami Dialecticae Libri Duo cum Commentariis. London, 1669. [The commentary is the same as that published separately in 1631.]

Einstein, Lewis. The Italian Renaissance in England. New York, 1902.

Gill, Alexander. Logonomia Anglica. Ed. by O. L. Jiriczek. Strassburg, 1903.

Graves, Frank P. Peter Ramus and the Educational Reformation of the Sixteenth Century. New York, 1912.

Greenlaw, Edwin. 'A Better Teacher than Aquinas,' SP. 14 (1917). 196-217.

'Spenser's Influence on *Paradise Lost*,' SP. 17 (1920). 320-59.

Grierson, Sir Herbert. Cross Currents in English Literature of the Seventeenth Century. London, 1929.

Hanford, James Holly. A Milton Handbook. New York, 1939.

'The Youth of Milton,' Studies in Shakespeare, Milton, and Donne. Ann Arbor, Michigan, 1925.

Langdon, Ida. Milton's Theory of Poetry and Fine Art. Cornell Studies in English, No. 8. New Haven, 1924.

Lewis, C. S. A Preface to *Paradise Lost*. London, 1942.

Lupton, Joseph H. A Life of John Colet. London, 1887.

Muirhead, John H. The Platonic Tradition in Anglo-Saxon Philosophy. London, 1931.

Nicolson, Marjorie H. 'The Spirit World of Milton and More,' SP. 22 (1925). 433-52.

Philo, with an English translation by F. H. Colson. Loeb Classical Library, London, 1937.

Saurat, Denis. La Pensée de Milton. Paris, 1920.

Schroeder, Kurt. Platonismus in der Englischen Renaissance vor und bei Thomas Eliot. Berlin, 1920.

Skeat, Walter, and E. H. Visiak. Milton's *Lament for Damon* and his Other Latin Poems. London, 1935.

Spaeth, Sigmund G. Milton's Knowledge of Music. Princeton, 1913.

Thompson, E. N. S. 'A Forerunner of Milton,' MLN. 32 (1917). 479-82.

Tulloch, John. Rational Theology and Christian Philosophy in England in the Seventeenth Century. Edinburgh, 1874.

Warren, William F. The Universe as Pictured in Milton's *Paradise Lost*. New York, 1915.

Watson, Foster. The English Grammar Schools to 1660. Cambridge, 1908.

COMMENTS ON THE RELATION OF MILTON AND PLATO, ARRANGED IN CHRONOLOGICAL SEQUENCE

Joseph Addison. The Spectator, No. 16. Works, ed. Richard Hurd. London, 1891. 2. 504.

William Hayley. The Life of Milton. London, 1796. Pp. 56-8, 206.

Samuel Taylor Coleridge. Letter to W. Sotheby, September 10, 1802. Letters, ed. by E. H. Coleridge. Boston, 1895. 1. 406.

Benjamin Jowett. 'The Genius of Plato,' Edinburgh Review 87 (1848). 321-67.

Alfred Stern. Milton und seine Zeit. Leipzig, 1877. 1. 115-7.

David Masson, ed. The Poetical Works of John Milton. London, 1890. 1. 178-9.

Charles Grosvenor Osgood. The Classical Mythology of Milton's English Poems. New York, 1900. Pp. xl-xli, lxx-lxxi.

John Smith Harrison. Platonism in English Poetry of the Sixteenth and Seventeenth Centuries. New York, 1903. Pp. 40-65, 82-3, 180-1.

Marianna Woodhull. The Epic of *Paradise Lost*. New York, 1907. Pp. 127, 312.

Alden Sampson. Studies in Milton. New York, 1913. Pp. 11-2, 243-305.

Sigmund Gottfried Spaeth. Milton's Knowledge of Music. Princeton, 1913. Pp. 15-6, 45, 66-7, 84-5, 97.

Evert Mordecai Clark, ed. *The Ready and Easy Way to Establish a Free Commonwealth* by John Milton. New Haven, 1915. Pp. xxxviii, lvii.

Lane Cooper. A Review of *Milton and Jakob Boehme* by Margaret Lewis Bailey. JEGP. 14 (1915). 290-6.

William Fairfield Warren. The Universe as Pictured in Milton's *Paradise Lost*. New York, 1915. Pp. 11, 14.

Edwin Greenlaw. 'A Better Teacher than Aquinas,' SP. 14 (1917). 196-217.

Robert L. Ramsay. 'Morality Themes in Milton's Poetry,' SP. 15 (1918). 123-58.

Elbert N. S. Thompson. 'Milton's *Of Education*,' SP. 15 (1918). 159-75.

James Holly Hanford. 'The Temptation Motive in Milton,' SP. 15 (1918). 176-94.

PLATO AND MILTON

'Milton and the Return to Humanism,' SP. 16 (1919). 126-47.

Edwin Greenlaw. 'Spenser's Influence on *Paradise Lost*,' SP. 17 (1920). 320-9.

Denis Saurat. La Pensée de Milton. Paris, 1920. Pp. 85, 274-5.

Edward Chauncey Baldwin. 'Milton and Plato's *Timaeus*,' PMLA. 35 (1920). 210-7.

Elbert N. S. Thompson. 'Mysticism in Seventeenth-Century English Literature,' SP. 18 (1921). 180-1, 191-2.

Herbert Agar. Milton and Plato. Princeton, 1928.

Oliver Morley Ainsworth. Milton on Education. New Haven, 1928. Pp. 43-5.

Ronald B. Levinson. 'Milton and Plato,' MLN. 46 (1931). 85-91.

E. M. W. Tillyard. Milton, Private Correspondence and Academic Exercises. Cambridge, 1932. Pp. xiii, xxvii, xxxiii- xxxiv.

Clara Starrett Gage. Sources of Milton's Concepts of Angels and the Angelic World. Cornell University dissertation, 1936. Pp. 137-9.

Merritt Y. Hughes, ed. John Milton, *Paradise Regained*, the Minor Poems, and *Samson Agonistes*. New York, 1937. Pp. xxxii-xxxiii, xlv, 411-2.

Clarence C. Green. 'The Paradox of the Fall in *Paradise Lost*,' MLN. 53 (1938). 557-71.

Josephine Waters Bennett. 'Milton's Use of the Vision of Er,' MP. 36 (1939). 351-8.

Don M. Wolfe. Milton in the Puritan Revolution. New York, 1941. P. 302.

Joseph Moody McDill. Milton and the Pattern of Calvinism. Vanderbilt University, Nashville, Tennessee, 1942. Pp. 121-3.

Index of Names and Titles

[*The Index includes proper names and titles, save that 'Milton,' 'Plato,' and 'Socrates' are omitted, and also the names and titles of publications found on pages 173-6.*]

INDEX

INDEX

INDEX

INDEX

INDEX